WAY TO GO!

SHOPPING IN SAN FRANCISCO

by
Carol Blackman
Diane Parente
Linda Farris

BUY THE BOOK ENTERPRISES

WAY TO GO!
SHOPPING
IN SAN FRANCISCO

by Carol Blackman, Diane Parente, Linda Farris

Cover by John Gompertz

Copyright © 1993 by Buy the Book Enterprises

All rights reserved. No part of this book may be reproduced in any form without the permission of Buy the Book Enterprises.

Printed and bound in the United States of America.

Published and distributed by:
    Buy the Book Enterprises
    P.O. Box 262
    Ross, CA 94957
    (415) 485-5250

ISBN: 0-9638673-0-X

DEDICATION:

To you, the shoppers . . .
(and to book buyers everywhere)

ACKNOWLEDGMENTS:

We'd like to acknowledge John Gompertz for his cover design, Dennis Woo for sharing his MAC expertise and Stephanie Peters for her graphic support. Thanks, too, to Jodie Chase for her excellent proofreading, Ellen Geisler for printing advice, Chuck Gompertz for his publishing know-how and Shirley Davalos for her marketing ideas and general handholding. And to all of our husbands and friends who put in their input, solicited and otherwise.

HOW TO USE THIS GUIDE

If you're looking for something specific, refer to the index.

If you're looking for a good time, and you have time to explore, check out the category headings for Union Square, Fisherman's Wharf, North Beach, Union Street and Hayes Valley, as well as the mentions, and decide where you want to start.

The map to your right will help you locate the major shopping areas. In the listings, note that each block begins with a grid indicating cross streets to help you locate the stores' exact locations, including side of the street. Restaurants and eateries are in *italics* in the grid and in the listings themselves, are identified with a coffee cup icon.

We've indicated one-way cab fares from Union Square, and where they exist, the bargain parking lots. You'll also find mentions of cable car routes, ferries, buses and Bay Area Rapid Transit (BART).

Here are some phone numbers which may come in handy:

> CITY CAB......................................468-7200
> YELLOW CAB............................626-2345
> MUNI (City Bus).......................673-6864
> BART...788-2278
> GOLDEN GATE FERRY............332-6600

CONTENTS

INTRODUCTION 10

UNION SQUARE/DOWNTOWN 12
    Sutter Street.. 13
    Post Street 27
    Maiden Lane 44
    Geary Street 48
    O'Farrell Street 57
    Grant Avenue 59
    Stockton Street 66
    Powell Street 72
    San Francisco Centre 76

THE WHARF 80
    Pier 39 82
    Along the Wharf 89
    The Cannery 91
    The Anchorage 93
    Ghirardelli Square 94

UNION STREET 96

NORTH BEACH 112
    Columbus Avenue 113
    Upper Grant Avenue 117

HAYES VALLEY 119

MENTIONS.. 126
   The Castro.. 126
   Embarcadero Center 127
   Fillmore.. 128
   Golden Gate Park 129
   The Haight.. 129
   Jackson Square....................................... 130
   Japantown... 131
   The Marina... 132
   The Mission.. 133
   Sacramento Street.................................. 134
   South of Market..................................... 136
   Stonestown Gallery 138

INDEX... 139

ABOUT THE AUTHORS

ORDER FORM

INTRODUCTION

We've been shopping in San Francisco all of our lives. Two of us, Carol and Diane, are natives. Linda, the new kid on the block, has been in town since 1969. Carol and Diane have been welcoming visitors to San Francisco and offering shopping advice to groups for years.

We looked for the perfect shopping guide to San Francisco for someone who only has a few days and wants to shop the best of San Francisco, from designer fashion, to unique gifts, to discount treasures.

We found nothing that was on target. The guidebooks told us too much, in type too small, in books too bulky.

Our audiences told us they wanted something easy to read, lightweight, fun and informative. So Diane and Carol sat down with Linda and her computer to create what we hope will be the answer to your shopping prayers.

You'll note that we've organized our guide by area, and by street and block. We've even told you where to stop for a cappuccino or a quick bite. Be sure to use the index in the back extensively. It has a life of its own and Linda has taken great care to cross-reference so everything you need will be at your fingertips.

Now, you're probably wondering how we kept this tome to under 2000 pages in one of the world's most renowned shopping meccas. It wasn't easy, but we were discriminating so you don't have to be.

You're getting the benefit of our opinions based on all that shopping experience we mentioned up there at the top. None of the stores listed here have paid to be included or had any input into what we had to say about them.

Do keep in mind that although we are updating this book annually, stores come and go, and sometimes they just move down the block. Please accept our blanket apology for absolutely any inconvenience we may have caused you in the past, present or future. And, yes, if you need to vent or have suggestions for us, please drop us a card to Buy the Book Enterprises, P.O. Box 262, Ross, CA 94957.

Because this book grew out of Carol and Diane's speaking about shopping and fashion, we want to remind you that if your convention or group would like to see us in action, we'd be delighted to hear from you. Check our bios in the back for more on our special professional presentations.

Now, get out those sensible shoes and a jacket in case the fog rolls in, and have the time of your life shopping San Francisco.

UNION SQUARE

Since 1850, Union Square has been the heart of downtown San Francisco and is the City's most famous shopping area. Union Square itself, a 2.6 acre park atop an underground garage, acquired its name during the Civil War, when it was the scene of mass rallies organized to support the Union cause. Union Square department stores, boutiques, hotels and historic buildings are concentrated in the surrounding five-block area.

Sutter Street

The 100 Block

	Kearny	
	Bentley's	B. Dalton Books
		Cafe Phoscao
	The Hound	U.S. Post Office
	Montgomery	

111 THE HOUND
Upscale men's traditional clothing, jazzier than Brooks Brothers.

150 U.S. POST OFFICE
The latest state-of-the-art stamps, including the new peel off, no-lick variety.

168 CAFE PHOSCAO ☕
And bar. Darling cafe for breakfast and lunch, open, bright and small. Good Italian energy.

185 BENTLEY'S ☕
Fresh seafood, oyster bar and Cajun dishes.

≈ **B. DALTON BOOKS**
At corner of Kearny & Sutter. Get a good look at San Francisco's financial district denizens who browse through lunch. A large selection of computer books and software downstairs.

Sutter Street

The 200 Block

	Grant
Joanie Char	A Pea in a Pod
	22 Steps
Doubleday Bookstore	Jeanne Marc
	Lascaux Bar & Rotisserie
	Cable Car Clothiers
	Loehmann's
	Cafe Claude
Wherehouse Records	Diana Slavin

Kearny

≈ **WHEREHOUSE RECORDS**
At corner of Kearny and Sutter. Hip hop on in for your tapes and compact discs.

≈ **DIANA SLAVIN**
3 Claude Alley (alley off Sutter next to Loehmann's). This San Francisco designer offers the look of women's Italian classics, using muted colors, luxurious fabrics and clean lines.

≈ **CAFE CLAUDE** ☕
Tucked away in Claude Alley next to Diana Slavin is this Parisian Bohemian cafe. Suggested attire: beret and anything black.

222 **LOEHMANN'S**
Two floors of discounted top designer women's fashions from Europe and New York.

14

Sutter Street

The 200 Block, continued

246 *CABLE CAR CLOTHIERS*
Traditional menswear, a San Francisco original as the name implies.

248 *LASCAUX BAR AND ROTISSERIE*
Step down into a cave for lunch if you can get in or a quick snack at the bar. Inspired by the cave paintings in France, Lascaux' ambiance is definitely worth the trip. Live jazz on weekend nights.

262 *JEANNE MARC*
Two San Francisco designers and fabricologists with a passion for quilted textures and bright colors offer whimsical loungewear for home entertaining, evening and cruise wear as well as accessories and home decor items. Their discount store south of Market at 508 3rd Street is open Tuesday through Saturday.

265 *DOUBLEDAY BOOKSTORE*
Books, books, books, books.... Bargains in the basement.

280 *22 STEPS*
If you want to stand out when you step out, this trend-setting store is your biscotti. If the shoe fits (and your credit card can foot the bill), wear it.

Sutter Street

The 200 Block, continued

285A *JOANIE CHAR*
This local designer creates colorful sportswear separates for women and sells them at wholesale prices at this downtown location.

290 *A PEA IN A POD*
Chic maternity wear.

Sutter Street

The 300 Block

	Stockton
Wilkes Bashford	Merrill's Drug Center
Joan Vass	Laise Adzer
Jessica McClintock	
Milano's Italian Kitchen	Ups and Downs
Health Foods	Petite Sophisticate
Composition Gallery	Michael's Art Supplies
Franciscan Croissant	
	Grant

301 FRANCISCAN CROISSANT ☕
Good people watching with a counter at the window, featuring speciality coffees, frozen yogurts, and, not surprisingly, croissants and croissant sandwiches.

314 MICHAEL'S ART SUPPLIES
More than an art supply store. Carol says it's a great place for pen junkies, from Waterman and Mont Blanc selections to antique fountain pens.

317 COMPOSITION GALLERY
Showcases contemporary glass art and designs in wood by more than 50 American and international artists.

333 HEALTH FOODS ☕
Healthy snacks while you sit at the counter. Our favorites: their yogurt shakes and apricot fruit bars. Wilkes Bashford likes the carrot-raisin salad.

Sutter Street

The 300 Block, continued

336 PETITE SOPHISTICATE
One of the few San Francisco stores that caters to petites.

340 UPS AND DOWNS
Discount children and junior fashions.

341 MILANO'S ITALIAN KITCHEN
California Italian cuisine at moderate prices. Great presentation of delicious pastas, salads and pizzas.

353 JESSICA McCLINTOCK
San Francisco designer specializing in feminine dresses and bridalwear. Fairytale, lacy Victorian look. (Her outlet warehouse south of Market at 35 Stanford at Brannan features fashions from past seasons at considerable savings.)

359 JOAN VASS
Daytime cotton cashmere knitwear.

360 LAISE ADZER INTERNATIONAL
Ethnic clothing with North African influence. Emphasis on drape and flow. One size fits all.

Sutter Street

The 300 Block, continued

375 ***WILKES BASHFORD***
Named for its founder, a legendary men's clothier, Wilkes Bashford offers six floors of luxury men's and women's European clothing as well as designs of local talent. They've recently added a homeware section featuring artisans from around the world.

390 ***MERRILL'S DRUG CENTER***
In the market for an original San Francisco band-aid for that blister, an aspirin for your head, Maalox for last night's dinner?

Sutter Street

The 400 Block

```
                    Stockton
        Rims & Goggles  | The Sherlock Holmes Museum
        Ann Taylor      | Pendleton
        Timberland      | Mrs. Field's Cookies
                        | Go Silk
                        | Maraolo Shoes
                        | Bogner
                    Powell
```

400 BOGNER
Quality German activewear for all seasons - from skiing to biking to golfing and tennis. Also carry separates in classy daywear.

404 MARAOLO SHOES
Stylish Italian men's and women's footwear. Also features last year's designs at a discount. Shares manufacturer with Armani, Donna Karen and DKNY.

424 GO SILK
Washable silks and linens for men and women.

428 MRS. FIELD'S COOKIES
Get your sugar high here.

437 TIMBERLAND
Rugged footwear to complement your Eddie Bauer ensemble. Hiking boots, clogs, sailing and walking shoes.

Sutter Street

The 400 Block, continued

441 ***ANN TAYLOR***
Stylish, upscale classics.

445 ***RIMS & GOGGLES***
Contemporary European and locally-designed eyewear. John Lennon would've shopped here.

464 ***PENDLETON***
Coveted classics of the '50s, known for women's plaid pleated skirts and men's plaid shirts at affordable prices.

480 ***THE SHERLOCK HOLMES MUSEUM***
(30th floor of the Holiday Inn) This cocktail lounge offers a light breakfast, a light dinner and a panoramic view in the midst of a collection of Sherlock Holmes artifacts.

Sutter Street

The 500 Block

Mason

Jeffrey Davies	Madrigal
La Bouquetiére	The Bookstall
Maxwell Galleries	*Orchard Garden Restaurant*
G.L. Morris	Boto USA, Inc.
Peking Arts - Antiques	Forgotten Woman
The Foreign Exchange	Three Bags Full
Kertesz	Smile Gallery
Ashling	Japanese Weekend
	Lori's Diner

Powell

500 LORI'S DINER AND BAKERY
A '50s soda fountain with black and white glossy interiors and a jukebox in the corner. Noted for their burgers, fries and dogs.

500 JAPANESE WEEKEND
Contemporary maternity clothes by local designers. Who says you can't be pregnant and stylish at the same time?

500 SMILE GALLERY
Dedicated to the glory of the imagination, it's whimsical, as its name suggests. Sculptures, ceramics, glass masks, clothing and accessories made by craftspeople with senses of humor.

Sutter Street

The 500 Block, continued

500 ***THREE BAGS FULL***
Quality handknit sweaters, colorful fun designs.

517 ***ASHLING***
Special one-of-a-kind gifts for you or your home. Cut-out magnetic paper dolls for your fridge and wire sculptures of hats, shoes and boots.

521 ***KERTESZ***
Fine art gallery. 19th and 20th century original European oil paintings.

527 ***THE FOREIGN EXCHANGE***
Exchange your dollars for foreign currency or vice versa. Add to your stamp and coin collections.

535 ***PEKING ARTS - ANTIQUES***
Wholesale and retail antique and new Chinese objets d'art.

541 ***G.L. MORRIS***
Vintage watches, jewelry and antiques.

Sutter Street

The 500 Block, continued

550 *FORGOTTEN WOMAN* Beautiful, with iron gate and garden in front. Stylish clothes for full figures from sizes 14 to 24. And they serve cookies to keep their customers coming back to this warm and friendly environment.

551 *MAXWELL GALLERIES* Fine collectible art. Historic American and California 19th and 20th century paintings from Hudson River School to American Impressionism.

556 *BOTO USA, INC.* Etched glass art and glass furniture.

562 *ORCHARD GARDEN RESTAURANT* Cubbyhole restaurant tucked away, using linens with breakfast and lunch.

563 *LA BOUQUETIERE* Country French home decor and accessories. You'll find wonderful gifts in this charming, friendly store.

570 *THE BOOKSTALL* Rare books and prints.

Sutter Street

The 500 Block, continued

575 *JEFFREY DAVIES*
Silk flower arrangements, antiques, floral art, table decor, great Christmas gifts and decorations.

590 *MADRIGAL*
Women's traditional sportswear, with a Carmel flavor.

The 600 Block

Taylor

Acad. of Art College Gallery
Marines Memorial Theatre
Mason

609 *MARINES MEMORIAL THEATRE*
For those shopping for tickets to original productions, be they native to San Francisco or off-Broadway.

625 *ACADEMY OF ART COLLEGE GALLERY*
Student artwork for sale.

Sutter Street

The 700 & 900 Blocks

Larkin
Wallis
Hyde

Leavenworth
Obiko
Argonaut Books
Sanraku
Taylor

704 *SANRAKU*
Japanese restaurant with the most reasonable sushi.

786 *ARGONAUT BOOKS*
A quiet shop stocked with rare and out-of-print books, prints, maps and manuscripts. A must for California history buffs.

794 *OBIKO*
Obiko offers one-of-a-kind fashions, most created by local designers, handpainted and handwoven. Obiko designs are carried by Bergdorf in New York. A rare find filled with treasures.

909 *WALLIS*
If you need exercise, hike up to this off-the-wall collection of hats, jewelry and homeware with a folk art influence.

Post Street

The First Block

Kearny
The Polo Store
Jay Briggs   The Crocker Galleria
Montgomery

50 *THE CROCKER GALLERIA*
Fashioned after the glass-domed Milan Galleria Vittorio Emmanuelle, this three tiered pavilion is a collection of 60 specialty shops, restaurants and services. You can pick up an international newspaper and a Mrs. Field's cookie while having your hair styled and shoes reheeled, all at the Galleria. And we've hardly mentioned shopping. Here are a few of our favorites:

CROCKER GALLERIA
LEVEL ONE

CRABTREE & EVELYN
Very Brit. English soaps and gifts, potpourri, skin care, dried flowers. Even jams. Great for custom gift baskets.

MONDI
Classic German dressy sportswear for women.

Post Street

The First Block, continued

CHURCH'S
British men's and women's shoes. Tip worth the price of this book: Their footware is less expensive here than in England, and you'll also save on airfare.

ARICIE LINGERIE DE MARQUE
Imports and fine silks.

CROCKER GALLERIA
LEVEL TWO

GIANNI VERSACE
Italian designs for men and women, slim cut, in three adjacent but distinct stores.

NICOLE MILLER
Ties, scarves, handbags, shoes, some apparel, all made from Nicole's conversational patterns, a story behind each one. Special designs for lawyers (gavels), Italians (pasta, olive oil, Chianti bottles), for the fashion monger, patterns with cosmetics or shoes. Great ice breakers for everyone from the timid to the attention-seeking extrovert.

Post Street

The First Block, continued

BROOKSTONE
Brookstone features practical new inventions for the man who has everything. Gifts, gadgets and tools. Almost like going to a museum.

PAPERMANIA
Specialty paper goods, gifts and cards.

CROCKER GALLERIA
LEVEL THREE

MARIMEKKO
Colorful women's clothing and table linens in block patterns - from Finland.

57 JAY BRIGGS
The ultimate preppy store for men, a San Francisco original. Chino pants, button-down shirts, a young Brooks Brothers for the thinner wallet.

90 THE POLO STORE
Ivy League sportswear for the well-bred man or woman designed by Ralph Lauren. Also features bed linens tucked in the back room.

Post Street

The 100 Block

	Grant
Scotch House	Coach Leathers
diPietro Todd	The North Face
Max Mara	Mark Cross
Tse Cashmere	Daniels & Wolfson
Celine	Williams Sonoma
	Episode
	Vidal Sassoon Salon
	Thomas Goldwasser
Hastings	Capezio
	Gap & Gap for Kids
	Kearny

100 *GAP & GAP FOR KIDS*
Cotton casual clothing for every generation. Fun matching t-shirts and socks.

101 *HASTINGS*
Men's and women's traditional suits galore.

126 *CAPEZIO*
2nd floor - Dance and costumewear, toeshoes, tapshoes, tights and leotards. Great for workout clothes.

126 *THOMAS GOLDWASSER*
Rare books and first additions.

130 *VIDAL SASSOON SALON*
Hair salon for the rich and famous.

Post Street

The 100 Block, continued

150 EPISODE
No frills classic clothing for women, similar designs to Calvin Klein or Armani, but more reasonably priced.

150 WILLIAMS-SONOMA
Kitchenware from around the world, a gourmet's delight. If you don't feel like schlepping, pick up their catalogue and shop from home.

150 DANIELS & WOLFSON
Suite 745. Dramatic jewelry. Design your own wedding ring.

155 CELINE
Elegant classic women's clothing. Madame Celine caters to the Grande Dames of Paris and San Francisco's ladies who lunch. We like her scarves.

170 MARK CROSS
The ultimate in status leather - handbags, luggage and accessories.

171 TSE CASHMERE
Cashmere clothing for women. (Cashmere, from the high-strung Kashmir goat, is the warmest of fabrics for the weight.)

Post Street

The 100 Block, continued

177 MAX MARA Women's Italian classic, yet fashionable clothing. The most stylist coats.

177 diPIETRO TODD 2nd floor - Full service salon - hair, massage, manicures and pedicures including Coreen Cordova's makeup studio for that special occasion. Will take walk-ins, or, the occasional shopping-weary limp-in.

180 THE NORTH FACE Two floors of outdoor clothing and accessories. A popular haunt for bicyclists, climbers and backpackers.

185 SCOTCH HOUSE Men and women's clothing and gifts, all from our friends far, far away.

190 COACH LEATHER American classic for 26 years. Sporty leather bags, briefcases and accessories which would have made Wild Bill Hickok sit up in his saddle. Their leather is heavy, lasts forever and is admired for its natural markings.

Post Street

The 200 Block

	Grant	
Florsheim Shoes		Alfred Dunhill
Escada		One Moment in Time
Sulka		Jaeger International
Laura Ashley		Gump's
American Express		Louis Vuitton
Cartier		Ciro
Burberry's Limited		Eddie Bauer
		Hats on Post
		The Shreve Building
Brooks Brothers		Shreve & Co.
	Stockton	

200 *SHREVE & CO.*
Fine jewelry, silver and crystal. Established in 1862, Shreve & Co. is the oldest retailer in San Francisco.

201 *BROOKS BROTHERS*
A branch of America's first store to sell ready-made clothing. This traditional clothing, shoes and accessory merchant has changed little since 1918. Quality and fair price.

210 *THE SHREVE BUILDING*
Don't be fooled by this historic building's office-like facade. You'll find a number of shops upstairs. Many are jewelers, some specializing in estate jewelry, and watch repair.

Post Street

The 200 Block, continued

210 *HATS ON POST*
2nd floor - Small hatbox of a store filled with a variety of hats for all occasions. Diane says that nothing changes one's look faster than a hat. The horizontal line of a brimmed hat does wonders for a long, narrow face. She says the fedora, cowboy and beret are the most popular hats of all time, but Carol and I think the baseball cap is a tad more popular, now stylishly worn backwards. In San Francisco in the '50s, a woman never deigned to venture downtown without her hat and gloves. If you're not sold on hats yet, Diane reminds us of the old adage, "If your feet are cold, put on a hat," and she swears by it.

220 *EDDIE BAUER*
Casual outdoor outfitter for men and women.

222 *CIRO*
Costume jewelry that resembles the real thing. A cozy store reminiscent of how service used to be. Sit on a tuffet and be served. This seems like a good place for one of Diane's tips: Never repeat the shape of your face in an earring.

Post Street

The 200 Block, continued

225 ***BURBERRY'S LIMITED***
Men's and women's traditional clothing from England: suits, shirts, coats. The unisex status symbol trench coat of all time was the Burberry, which is now available in colors other than tan. Picture Bogie fading into the fog at the end of "Casablanca."

230 ***LOUIS VUITTON***
Status French handbags and luggage. Carol, who has met Louis' great grandson in this very store and brags that she drank champagne with him, says the Parisian concern is still family run. They are world renowned for making custom luggage. Napoleon had them make a trunk for him that converted to a bed.

231 ***CARTIER***
Conveniently located for Francophiles across from Vuitton, Cartier, the famous jeweler, is known for his popular tank watch and rolling rings, bands of white, rose and yellow gold, designed by Cartier himself in 1924.

237 ***AMERICAN EXPRESS***
You say you're here in this shopping mecca and you left home without it?

Post Street

The 200 Block, continued

250 **GUMP'S**
This original San Francisco store, doubling as a museum, got its start in the Gold Rush era selling mirrors to the city's famous bordellos and saloons. Our favorite way to "do" Gumps is to start at the jade room on the top floor and wend your way down through the furniture, fine art, Baccarat crystal (some of which was commissioned for royalty) china, silver, home decor, lovely gifts, fine jewelry and stationery. Gump's holiday windows in recent years have featured irresistable puppies and kittens up for adoption from our local humane society. All three of us agree, Gump's is a must-see at any time of the year.

253 **LAURA ASHLEY**
Laura has turned classic. Added to her romantic floral prints are softly-tailored blazers and skirts with a feminine touch. She also offers English country fabrics, wallpaper and sheets.

255 **SULKA**
Men's haberdasher -- shirts, ties, suspenders, everything but the suit.

Post Street

The 200 Block, continued

259 ESCADA
The Mercedes of fashion. German dressy classics for the elegant woman. Known for their distinctive motifs, such as jackets covered with decals or buttons. Escada is an example, says Carol, of San Francisco's wonderful shopping environment where so many European shops are clustered in a small geographical area.

272 JAEGER INTERNATIONAL
This English store features traditional women's timeless fashions (sizes 6-18) celebrated for their beautiful fabrics and workmanship. Clothes that last a lifetime. Remember that you're one size larger in English clothing. Last season's fashions at a reduced rate are downstairs.

278 ONE MOMENT IN TIME
Upstairs in Suite 404. Designer evening gown rentals at 25% of the purchase price in sizes 4 to 22. They'll even provide matching purses and jewelry. You can reserve up to 60 days in advance.

Post Street

The 200 Block, continued

290 **ALFRED DUNHILL OF LONDON**
Another upscale Brit store featuring clothing and accessories for the elegant gentleman. Check out the Humidor Room, temperature controlled for prized cigars and pipe tobacco.

299 **FLORSHEIM SHOES**
Substantial, basic shoes for men.

Post Street

The 300 Block

```
                    Powell
                            Saks Fifth Avenue
         UNION SQUARE       Tiffany & Co.
                            Bullock & Jones
                    Stockton
```

340 *BULLOCK & JONES*
This purveyor of fine British clothing for men and women has been purveying since 1853. Veeerrrry conventional.

350 *TIFFANY & CO.*
There's more to Tiffany's than breakfast. This New York jeweler is known for the Tiffany setting of a single round brilliant cut diamond perched on prongs for all to admire. And there are gifts, believe it or not, for under $50.

384 *SAKS FIFTH AVENUE*
This classy New York specialty store has a well edited selection of upscale apparel and accessories for the entire family. Sophisticated career wear that works. This is one of the few stores in San Francisco where you can order or purchase a couture designer outfit. Take time to have a complimentary makeup lesson in their notable cosmetic department. Enjoy the view of Union Square from the cafe on the top floor.

Post Street

The 400 Block

```
                    Mason
                    The Ritz Deli
                    La Parisienne
                    Theatre on the Square
                    Joseph Rudee & Son
                    Bazaar Cada Dia
                    Caffe Classico
                    Gallery 444
     My Sister's Garden    Swaine Adeney
                    Powell
```

427 *MY SISTER'S GARDEN* Colorful decorative Italian pottery for kitchen and patio.

434 *SWAINE ADENEY* The only Swaine Adeney in the U.S., they have fine English country and equestrian items, not to mention their bumpershoots. The whip and glove makers to Queen Elizabeth. Sounds like fun.

444 *GALLERY 444* Contemporary folk art.

448 *CAFFE CLASSICO* ☕ Best lattes and gelato in the area. Open at 7:30 a.m.

Post Street

The 400 Block, continued

448 BAZAAR CADA DIA
Gifts from around the world. Ethnic art and jewelry from American Indian to East African cultures, with a little Russian, Far East, Turkish, South American thrown in. The United Nations of bazaars.

450 JOSEPH RUDEE & SON
Inside the Kensington Park Hotel - Custom, made-to-measure shirt makers.

450 THEATRE ON THE SQUARE
Inside the Kensington Park Hotel - An 800-seat theatre offering quality off-Broadway shows.

460 LA PARISIENNE
French costume jewelry in a boutique reminiscent of the late 1800's, specializing in art deco and art nouveau historic pieces and current French designs. Collectibles from the late 1800 and early 1900 era, including French posters on linen and Limoge boxes.

470 THE RITZ DELI
A real deli with no seating.

Post Street

The 500 & 600 Blocks

Jones
China Moon Cafe
Taylor
Harold's Hometown News
Postrio
Mason

545 ***POSTRIO*** ☕ The four-star restaurant features contemporary California cuisine with haute prices. Have a Wolfgang Puck pizza at the bar, without a reservation.

599 ***HAROLD'S HOMETOWN NEWS*** Magazines and newspapers from out-of-state and around the world.

639 ***CHINA MOON CAFE*** ☕ American diner turned Chinese bistro with deco-style appointments. Famous for stir-fry and original booths from the '30s. For a quick bite, sit at the counter.

Post Street

The 700 to 900 Blocks

	Larkin	
		Zinc Details
	Hyde	
		MAC
	Leavenworth	
		Ed Hardy San Francisco, Inc.
		The John Pence Gallery
	Jones	

750 *THE JOHN PENCE GALLERY* Features American realism paintings, past and present.

750 *ED HARDY SAN FRANCISCO, INC.* Frequented by interior designers and New Yorkers, Ed specializes in 17th and 18th century English and French antiques.

812 *MAC* It stands for Modern Appeal Clothing, very Soho - trendy and hip. They even have bejeweled collars for your pooch or puss.

906 *ZINC DETAILS* One-of-a-kind furniture created by artists, contempary glassware, bud vases and lamps. Barney's of New York buys here.

Maiden Lane

This elegant tree-lined alley extends two blocks east of Union Square. In the heyday of the Barbary Coast, it was called Morton Street and it was lined with houses of ill repute. The ladies of the evening were moved out as the boutiques replaced the bordellos.

The First Block

	Grant	
Nosheria		Candlelier
		Métier
McHugh & Co.		Orientations
	Kearny	

33 McHUGH & CO.
Local designer creates classics with pizazz. Coordinates that are easy to wear and accessorize.

34 ORIENTATIONS
Antiques and Asian art.

50 METIER
Soho on Maiden Lane. Clothes for artists or wannabes (with visible means of support) by young international designers. Sophisticated and graphic designs.

Maiden Lane

The First Block, continued

60 ***CANDLELIER***
Artichoke and apple candles, and that's just the A's. Also, tableware for all occasions.

69. ***NOSHERIA*** ☕
Cute deli with outside seating in good weather.

Maiden Lane

The 100 Block

Stockton
Spectacles
Dreamweaver
Chanel
Robison's Pets   The Circle Gallery
Zantman Art Galllery   Pierre Deux
Grant

111 *ZANTMAN ART GALLERY*
Representational paintings and sculpture by living artists.

120 *PIERRE DEUX*
Country French fabrics, home furnishing and accessories.

135 *ROBISON'S PETS*
Quality pet supplies and accessories established in 1849. Adorable.

140 *THE CIRCLE GALLERY*
Step into a living sculpture in this 1948 landmark Frank Lloyd Wright building. The spiral ramped showroom features contemporary art, limited editions of Erte silkscreens and jewelry, and paper sculpture by Gallo (not the wine guy).

Maiden Lane

The 100 Block, continued

155 CHANEL
Chanel is, of course, Coco Chanel's legacy. The Parisian designer never married and used her romantic attachments to inspire her fashion creations. The legendary Chanel suit has, with the exception of skirt length and shoulder width, maintained its look and dignity for fifty years. Still considered an excellent clothing investment. Chanel is also known for perfume, shoes and handbags.

173 DREAMWEAVER
Unique handknit sweaters from around the world.

177 SPECTACLES
Great eyewear for all faces. Known for their famous face furniture. Hint: Select a shape other than your face shape, i.e. angled frame for a round face, rounded frame for a square face. A nasty designer once told Linda that with her long narrow face and beady eyes, she needed frames that would pull her eyes apart.

Geary Street

Downtown Geary Street is gallery row so Diane feels a couple of definitions are in order. Today, contemporary art isn't something produced by our contemporaries necessarily. It is interpretive art, left to your imagination. It's not objective art. You don't have to get it, you just have to appreciate it, or not. Representational art is realistic art. What you see is what you get.

The First Block

Grant

Anthony's Shoe Service	Michael Duney Gallery
	Rena Branstein Gallery
	Fraenkel Gallery
	Stephen Wirtz Gallery
Gallery Paule Anglim	Haines Gallery

Kearny

14 GALLERY PAULE ANGLIM
Celebrated contemporary American artists and emerging artists are showcased.

30 ANTHONY'S SHOE SERVICE
A full service shoe repair shop.

Geary Street

The First Block, continued

49 *HAINES GALLERY*
Three distinct galleries at 49 Geary all feature contemporary art. Haines specializes in sculpture, photography, painting, drawings, and installation art. (They create environments.)

49 *STEPHEN WIRTZ GALLERY*
Wirtz features post-1945 contemporary Bay Area, New York and international artists.

49 *FRAENKEL GALLERY*
And Fraenkel presents 19th and 20th century photography.

77 *RENA BRANSTEIN GALLERY*
Sculpture, painting, photography, video!

77 *MICHAEL DUNEV GALLERY*
Painting, photography and sculpture by emerging and established artists.

Geary Street

The 100 Block

```
                    Grant
        Neiman Marcus   North Beach Leather
                        Joan & David
                        Naturalizer
                        Betsey Johnson
                        Paul Bauer Inc.
                        Britex Fabrics
                        Jacqueline DeBray
               Talbots  James Osswald
Mother's Work Maternity  N. Peal Cashmere
                        Bottega Veneta
                   Stockton
```

108 *BOTTEGA VENETA*
Italian handbags, soft as butter. Fine quality shoes, scarves, ties and luggage.

110 *N. PEAL CASHMERE*
Colorful assortment of sweaters for men and women, as well as blazer crests, sets of buttons and cashmere socks. (Use Ivory Snow or Woolite and add a capful of ammonia to the water to prevent graying.)

125 *MOTHER'S WORK MATERNITY*
Feminine maternity clothes.

129 *TALBOTS*
Traditional clothing and accessories for women, including petite sizes.

Geary Street

The 100 Block, continued

140 *JAMES OSSWALD*
Luggage and handbag repair. Quick turn-around.

140 *JACQUELINE DeBRAY*
6th floor - French design studio specializing in blouses, coordinates, and dresses and even dresses for bridesmaids and mother of the bride. Choice of ready to wear or Jacqueline's own unique designs.

146 *BRITEX FABRICS*
The most extensive fabric store ever, down to and including feather boas, masks, silk flowers and wedding accessories. The notions department is famous for their buttons of every color and variety. You can even make earrings out of them! Try the remnant floor for great bargains.

156 *PAUL BAUER INC.*
Fine china and crystal, most complete selection of German China and Royal Delph.

160 *BETSEY JOHNSON*
Far-out women's clothing. Young, space age and inexpensive. Carol says Betsey made her reputation with lycra.

Geary Street

The 100 Block, continued

170 **NATURALIZER**
Shoes for feet with an attitude, from narrow to wide. Comfort and practicality reign.

172 **JOAN & DAVID**
Men's and women's fashion shoes, handbags, accessories, and a limited selection of women's coordinates.

190 **NORTH BEACH LEATHER**
Modern leather clothing for men and women.

≈ **NEIMAN MARCUS**
At corner of Geary & Stockton. Famous Dallas purveyor of upscale merchandise from couture designer wear to moderate sportswear for women, men and children. Also known for their own line of gourmet foods and other unique gifts. They carry Joseph Schmidt's Chocolates, the best truffles in town. Located in the old City of Paris venue, the original stained glass dome is worth a visit and the Rotunda Restaurant on the 4th floor is perfect for afternoon tea and offers an excellent perch over Union Square.

Geary Street

The 200 Block

```
              Powell
           Imposters
        Bruno Magli   UNION SQUARE
             Macy's
           I. Magnin
             Stockton
```

~ I. MAGNIN

At Stockton. An elegant San Francisco tradition. Mary Ann Magnin founded the store in 1876 offering fine lingerie to the fine ladies of the day, or the night. Today, I. Magnin offers upscale clothing and accessories for men and women and an expanded gift department. The sixth floor, called "A New Attitude," is a boutique within the store, offering trendy New York Soho garb. Stop in the basement for lunch or to accessorize your sweet tooth at Narsai's Cafe.

~ MACY'S

With entrances on Geary, Stockton and O'Farrell, Macy's is San Francisco's largest department store. One stop shopping, a store for all sizes, personalities and lifestyles. The largest selection of petite and full figure fashions. Macy's basement is famous for its fresh deli fare, variety of sweets and Wolfgang Puck's fabulous pizza as well as a U.S. Postal Service branch open seven days a week. The men's store, across the street at 120 Stockton, also carries children's clothing, luggage and electronics.

Geary Street

The 200 Block, continued

285 BRUNO MAGLI
This is the Ferrari of footwear for fashionable men and women.

295 IMPOSTERS
Fabulous fake jewelry worn by the stars.

The 300 Block

Mason
Casual Corner | Mama's
Powell

301 CASUAL CORNER
Fashionable women's attire at an equally casual price. Easy to build a wardrobe around these mix and match coordinates. Tiptime from Diane: Start with a jacket, next find the skirts/pants, and add two to three tops per bottom.

398 MAMA'S
One of a chain of San Francisco eateries founded by Mama Sanchez. Open all day for traditional American fare, they make their own jams and breads daily.

Geary Street

The 400 Block

```
                    Taylor
                           Ann Michaels
       The Curran Theatre  David's
       The Geary Theatre   The California Pizza Kitchen
                    Mason
```

415 *THE GEARY THEATRE*
This home of San Francisco's famous American Conservatory Theatre was a victim of the Great Quake of 1989, and has yet to reopen.

445 *THE CURRAN THEATRE*
This elegant San Francisco theatre, opened in 1922, is home to the "Best of Broadway" series.

438 *THE CALIFORNIA PIZZA KITCHEN* ☕
Chrome, steel, great pizza and grilled veggies.

468 *DAVID'S* ☕
Since 1952, a deli to warm the lox and bagels of a New Yorker's heart. Great macaroons and New York cheesecake.

486 *ANN MICHAELS*
Charming small store brimmed with treasures, gifts and antiques for all pocketbooks.

Geary Street

The 500 Block

Taylor
City of Paris
Jones

≈ ***CITY OF PARIS*** ☕
Shannon Alley off Geary. The entrance to this European bistro is tucked away on the side of the El Cortez Hotel. Open for lunch and dinner, you'll find California-French cuisine. We recommend the open faced chicken sandwich.

O'Farrell Street

※

The First & 100 Blocks

Powell
| The Ellis O'Farrell Garage | Macy's |
Stockton
| *The Orchard Inn* | |
| The Tall Shop | |
Grant

61 ***THE TALL SHOP***
Women's clothing for those 5'11" to 6'3". Coats, suits, separates and casual wear.

75 ***THE ORCHARD INN***
A little European coffee shop seating some 25. Breakfast, lunch and great creamed spinach.

≈ ***MACY'S***
This entrance to Macy's lands you smack dab in the middle of makeup and jewelry. See Macy's blurb in the 200 block of Geary.

123 ***THE ELLIS O'FARRELL GARAGE***
One of the best deals in town for short-term parking, under three hours.

O'Farrell Street

The 200 Block

Powell
Corona Bar & Grill   The Handlery Union Sq. Hotel
Stockton

260 **THE HANDLERY UNION SQ. HOTEL**
If you're looking for the best long-term parking deal in the Union Square area, you can park for up to 12 hours for a mere $8 - a steal in this berg - if you get in by 10 a.m.

CORONA BAR & GRILL
At corner of Cyril Magnin Place and Ellis - Now this gets confusing, but we don't want you walking down Ellis Street. Not the best area. So continue walking up O'Farrell, turning left on Cyril Magnin Place between Powell and Mason. One block down on the left, you'll find our favorite California Mexican cuisine at the Corona Bar & Grill. Have a margarita and a quick bite at the bar.

Grant Avenue

This picturesque avenue stretches from Market Street through the enclave of the largest Chinese settlement outside of China.

The First Block

Geary
Overland Sheepskin Co.
Emporio Armani
O'Farrell

1 EMPORIO ARMANI
Enter the Italian world of fashion. Elegant modern classics for men and women. The edifice used to be one of the city's most prestigious banks. Today, you can take a shopping break to sip wine at the espresso bar in the center of the store, or enjoy a more formal meal upstairs on the balcony overlooking the designer goods below.

21 OVERLAND SHEEPSKIN CO.
Fleece-lined sheepskin and leather clothing for both sexes in this Western movie-set-of-a-shop.

Grant Avenue

The 100 Block

```
                    Post
      Crate & Barrel | Light Opera Gallery
         Frank More  | St. Croix
                   Geary
```

105 *FRANK MORE*
Modern shoes for men and women.

125 *CRATE & BARREL*
Simple, functional kitchen and patio ware with style. Outfits your home like the Gap outfits you. Gap homeworld.

164 *ST. CROIX*
Cotton and wool sweaters for men and women patterned after art. (The Bill-Cosby-incomfortable-sweater look.)

174 *LIGHT OPERA GALLERY*
A little bit of Russia in San Francisco. Gifts and art glass. Specialties include Russian lacquer boxes, paperweights and dolls.

Grant Avenue

The 200 Block

Sutter

Tillman Bookstore	Banana Republic
Geordy's	John Berggruen Gallery
LaBelle	Malm
	Moss Gallery
	Tom Wing & Sons

Post

208 *TOM WING & SONS*
Chinese family jeweler specializing in jade, pearls and gold.

214 *MOSS GALLERY*
Fine art, contemporary Latin paintings.

222 *MALM*
Need several extra suitcases for your new purchases? Malm offers high-end luggage, business and office accessories.

228 *JOHN BERGGRUEN GALLERY*
Contemporary art, 20th century American, European paintings, sculpture, drawings and prints.

233 *LaBELLE*
Treat the face, hands and feet to a facial, manicure and pedicure.

Grant Avenue

The 200 Block, continued

≈ **GEORDY'S**
1 Tillman Place, a small, cozy brick alley on the west side of the 200 block of Grant. This is the new "in" restaurant. Innovative French Mediterranean food. Pricey.

≈ **TILLMAN BOOKSTORE**
8 Tillman Place. Small but discriminating. Known for their selection of histories and biographies.

256 BANANA REPUBLIC
From safari to upscale Gap look. Elegant weekend separates.

Grant Avenue

The 300 Block

```
            Bush
            Cafe de la Presse
            S.F. Dragonflys & Co.
            Don Sherwood
            Sutter
```

320 ***DON SHERWOOD***
Golf and tennis clothing and accessories.

334 ***S.F. DRAGONFLYS & CO.***
Tiffany reproduction lamps. Art deco and Nouveau style lamps and light fixtures.

352 ***CAFE DE LA PRESSE*** ☕
In this European-style cafe, you'll find newspapers and magazines from around the world and maps to help you get your bearings or plan your next adventure.

Grant Avenue
The 400 Block & Up

Chinatown

At Bush and Grant, enter Chinatown through the famous Chinese welcome gate, and mingle with the 80,000 residents who inhabit these 18 square blocks. You can buy silk by the yard, whole sets of china, small flat black slippers or a silk jacket with knotted buttons. Diane likes the Battenberg Lace style comforter covers, sheets and pillow shams for her bedroom. You'll also find great beaded tops or appliqué pins that dress up sweaters and jackets.

Gifts to bring home include hand-painted bookmarks with Chinese scenes, silk eyeglass cases and coin purses, cloisonné pillboxes and pens, Christmas ornaments, Chinese motif pot holders and sandalwood soap.

Helpful hints: Compare prices. They will vary from store to store. Many shops accept credit cards or cash but no personal checks. For the adventuresome, venture into an herb shop. You'll probably catch the herbalist figuring the bill on an abacus.

Grant Avenue
The 400 Block & Up

The Chinese food markets are equally fascinating. And if you're ready to try an authentic Chinese lunch and do battle with chopsticks, look for the word "dim sum," which means "little jewel" in Chinese. Dim sum restaurants serve a host of Chinese finger foods. The language barrier shouldn't present a problem, as the servers wheel around carts of bite-size treats and you simply point to the ones you'd like to try.

If you're curious about the future, you'll find fortune cookies by the bag at the Golden Gate Fortune Cookie Factory at 56 Ross Alley, parallel to Grant, off Jackson Street.

Stockton Street

The First Block

	O'Farrell	
Limited Express	F.A.O. Schwarz	
	Ghirardelli Chocolate	
	Ellis	

44 **_GHIRARDELLI CHOCOLATE_**
If you can't make it to Ghirardelli Square, you'll find these delectably delicious and legendary chocolates of San Francisco right here as well as San Francisco souvenirs.

48 **_F.A.O. SCHWARZ_**
Welcome to San Francisco's Disneyland, world-renowned toy store from New York. You're greeted by a toy soldier doorman. A great place for children and adults to play, you'll find a selection ranging from a simple game of marbles to life-sized stuffed animals and miniature versions of classic sports cars you can drive out the door past that toy soldier doorman.

55 **_LIMITED EXPRESS_**
Women's sportswear and separates. The latest trends at a good price.

Stockton Street

The 100 Block

```
           Geary
    I. Magnin  Neiman Marcus
              Macy's
          O'Farrell
```

120 *MACY'S*
This is Macy's headquarters for menswear, the children's department, luggage and electronics. Across the street from the larger store. (See listing in the 200 block of Geary.)

135 *I. MAGNIN*
Our elegant department store. (See listing in 200 block of Geary.)

150 *NEIMAN MARCUS*
The famous Dallas store. (See listing in 100 block of Geary.)

Stockton Street

The 200 Block

	Post
	Bally of Switzerland
UNION SQUARE	Arthur Beren
STBS	Hermes
	Gucci
	Geary

200 *GUCCI*
Men's and women's fine clothing, shoes and accessories in this status symbol store made famous in the '70s. Known for the Gucci loafers and the red and green striped handbags with double Gs.

212 *HERMES*
San Francisco's version of the famous Parisian royal saddle and harness maker since 1837. Hermes gave birth to the Kelly bag, named for the elegant Princess Grace of Monaco, for whom the bag was created. Silk scarves and men's ties are made of patterns with as many as 22 different colors. Jackie O frames some of her Hermes scarves as art. This is investment dressing.

222 *ARTHUR BEREN*
Two floors of men's and women's classic shoes, including a large selection of Ferragamo, Cole Haan, Mephisto and Arche.

Stockton Street

The 200 Block, continued

238 ***BALLY OF SWITZERLAND***
High quality European shoes and leather goods for men and women.

STBS
STBS stands for San Francisco Ticket Box Office Service and is a walk-up booth right on Union Square. You can purchase full-price tickets or tickets at half-price (plus a nominal service charge) on the day of the performance to selected events. No phone orders, no refunds. Cash only. Open noon to 5 p.m., Tuesdays through Saturdays.

Stockton Street

The 300 Block

Sutter
- Janot's
- Bulgari
- Scheuer Linens
- Wedgewood & Waterford

Post

304 ***WEDGEWOOD & WATERFORD***
A complete selection of china and crystal from the British Isles.

318 ***SCHEUER LINENS***
Large European collection of bed, bath and table linens. They specialize in monogramming.

340 ***BULGARI***
(in the Campton Place Hotel-Kempinski) - One of the finest jewelry stores in the world, founded in Rome in 1884. Famous for stylized gold and silver jewelry.

≈ ***JANOT'S***
At 44 Campton Place Alley, a cozy French bistro for lunch.

Stockton Street

The 400 Block

	Bush
	The Sutter Stockton Garage
	Sutter

~ THE SUTTER-STOCKTON GARAGE

This and the O'Farrell Street garage are the best short-term parking deals in the downtown area. If you are staying less than three hours, you'll pay only a couple of dollars. However, after three hours, the rates jump dramatically. You can enter this garage on Stockton Street or from an entrance into Level Four from Bush Street.

Powell Street

❧❦❧

It's at the foot of Powell Street at Market that San Francisco's famous little cable cars begin their climb halfway to the stars. Street vendors and entertainers congregate at the cable car turnaround. Other characters at this corner aren't quite as entertaining and don't have anything to sell, but they'd still like to share the wealth, so hang onto your treasures.

❧❦❧

The 100 Block

O'Farrell
| Hunter's Bargain Bookstore | |
| Walgreen Drug Store | Books, Inc. |
Ellis

135 *WALGREEN DRUG STORE*
You say you need aspirin? Film? Or a foldable luggage carrier for your new purchases? Duck into Walgreens.

140 *BOOKS, INC.*
Well-stocked bookstore, noted for their cookbooks.

151 *HUNTER'S BARGAIN BOOKSTORE*
Bargain books on every topic.

Powell Street

The 200 & 300 Blocks

```
                    Post
        Victoria's Secret   UNION SQUARE
                    Geary
        Casual Corner
        Caffe Kuleto's
        Kuleto's
                  O'Farrell
```

221 KULETO'S ☕
A favorite downtown Italian restaurant with yummy pastas and stuffed chicken.

227 CAFFE KULETO'S ☕
A mini-take-out cafe with fresh innovative fare. Great sandwiches. Yummy homemade gelatos and sorbettos. And yes, vegetarians will feel right at home here.

～ CASUAL CORNER
Corner of Powell & Geary - Women's separates sportswear. (See listing at 301 Geary Blvd.)

335 VICTORIA'S SECRET
Located in the St. Francis Hotel, this boudoir environment features women's intimate apparel and bath accoutrements - look it up, it's French! Rekindle a flame or light a new fire. This is THE place to buy sexy underwear.

Powell Street

The 400 Block

```
              Sutter
              Galina
      Bank of America   Uni
              Sears     Saks Fifth Avenue
              Post
```

≈ SAKS FIFTH AVENUE
At the corner of Post and Powell. Classy New York import. (See listing at 384 Post.)

439 SEARS ☕
This San Francisco institution since the Great Fire of '06 serves a good breakfast at a good price, all-American comfort food. The decor is strictly 1940s coffeeshop motif.

445 BANK OF AMERICA
Need some cash from a B. of A. Versateller?

450 UNI
A gem of a store offering great sweater jackets. Look for their all-purpose angora sweater coat that can compete with any mink.

457 GALINA
Glittery faux jewels from this London designer. Galina supplies Dame Edna with her outrageous jewels and eyewear. Other famous clients: Princess Di and Joan Collins.

Powell Street

The 500 Block

Bush
Double Rainbow
Sutter

519 *DOUBLE RAINBOW* ☕
Would it be worth climbing a bit higher up Nob Hill for an ice cream cone, piece of fudge or carrot cake? Carol thinks so. If you don't like to start with dessert, try their sandwiches or quiche.

San Francisco Shopping Centre

At 865 Market, across from the Cable Car turnaround at the foot of Powell, is our favorite vertical mall, the San Francisco Shopping Centre. Completed in 1988, this nine-floor enclosed collection of shops is anchored by Nordstrom, the Seattle-based retailer. Many visitors whip out their cameras to capture the spectacular circular escalator that spirals between the levels.

Pick up a complete store listing at the information desk on the Street Level and study it over a French pastry and coffee at La Nouvelle Patisserie, also on the Street Level. Our listings here single out some of our favorite San Francisco Centre stores:

STREET LEVEL

JEWELRY STOP
An impressive selection of creative earrings and pins created by Lunch at the Ritz. Whimsical theme earrings with dangling charms.

AS TIME GOES BY
Vintage watches, jewelry and art deco accessories.

San Francisco Shopping Centre

continued

EMPORIUM
One of San Francisco's historic department stores, with entrances on the street level of the San Francisco Centre and from Market Street. You'll find everything here, from cosmetics to apparel for the whole family.

EL PORTAL
Luggage for the world traveler.

WARNER BROS.
Movie memorabilia, t-shirts and gifts. Look for the Bogart/Bacall "Here's Looking at You" t-shirt.

ADRIENNE VITTADINI
Women's clothing, colorful knits and separates.

MONDI
German designed classic clothes for women.

I.B. DIFFUSION
Novelty sweaters and jackets for women.

CENTRE LEVEL 2

BEBE
Dramatic day and evening wear for women. Slim bodies required.

San Francisco Shopping Centre

continued

MUSIC BOX COMPANY
Magical novelty boxes that sing to you. They will personalize music boxes with your special song.

HOLD EVERYTHING
Closet, business and kitchen organizers.

WILLIAMS-SONOMA
Quality kitchenware. (See listing at 150 Post.)

CACHE
Creative dramatic women's clothing. Jazzy day and evening wear. Watch for beading, sequins and appliqué.

CENTRE LEVEL 3

J CREW
Casual weekend wear in natural fibers for men and women.

AUDREY JONES
Full-figured women's clothes.

ANN TAYLOR
Dressy separates for women.

VICTORIA'S SECRET
Women's sexy lingerie.

San Francisco Shopping Centre

continued

MOSAIC GALLERY
Contemporary Bay Area artists. Ceramics and embossed prints.

LES ENFANTS
One-of-a-kind children's wear.

NINE WEST
Comfortable, stylish shoes at a fair price.

HARRY MASON DESIGN STUDIO
Innovative handmade gold and silver earrings by a California designer. Lightweight and nickel-free.

CENTRE LEVEL 4

NORDSTROM
Nordstrom starts on the fourth level of the center, but they call this Nordstrom Level 1. Go figure. Noted for the largest shoe selection in town, if they don't have it, they'll get it. This is a great place to get your basics -- blouses, sweaters, skirts and pants in all colors. Shop all four levels of Nordstrom, stop for refreshment in any of their four restaurants and take time to be revitalized in the Nordstrom Spa on the store's top floor.

FISHERMAN'S WHARF

San Francisco's colorful Fisherman's Wharf was born at the turn of the century when the state set aside the waterfront between Taylor and Leavenworth Streets as a dock for commercial fishing boats. Industrious Italian fishermen, in addition to selling some of their catch to neighborhood housewives, began to offer clam chowder to passers-by. Soon they expanded their sidewalk menu to include crab and shrimp cocktails. And the advent of Thousand Island dressing yielded the Wharf's most popular dish, Crab Louie.

With the development of Pier 39, Ghirardelli Square and the Cannery, Fisherman's Wharf has become a shopper's paradise. Combined with restaurants and entertainment, it's little wonder that the Wharf is San Francisco's number one tourist destination.

In addition to the Ripley's Believe It or Not! Museum and the Guinness Museum of World Records, you'll find a variety of art galleries stretching the length of the waterfront.

We're going to work our way from east to west, starting at the oh-so-popular Pier 39.

FISHERMAN'S WHARF

⇒|⇐

GETTING THERE: A taxi ride from Union Square to the Wharf one-way will cost about $6. The Powell/Hyde cable car ($2 each way) will take you to Hyde at Beach Streets, between the Cannery and Ghirardelli Square. The Powell/Mason cable car line ends at Mason and Bay, just a couple blocks walk from the Wharf and five or six blocks from Pier 39. The #30 Stockton bus will also bring you to the edge of Wharf. Pier 39 and Ghirardelli have parking garages which offer validation, but are still pricey.

Pier 39

The third most popular attraction in the world (after Disney World and Disneyland), Pier 39 draws ten-and-a-half million visitors a year. The 45-acre festival marketplace boasts more than 100 one-of-a-kind shops, restaurants, attractions, a 350-berth marina and some of the City's best views of the Bay, the Golden Gate Bridge, and Alcatraz.

In January 1990, Pier 39's West Marina was adopted by a few dozen California sea lions who claimed the docks as their own. Supported by the Bay's plentiful herring supply, the sea lion population at the Pier has grown to an impression 600 and became a natural attraction that added to the Pier's popularity. Now, Pier 39, in conjunction with The Marine Mammal Center, supply docents to provide information on the playful pinnipeds each weekend from 11 am to 5 pm.

Visitors to Pier 39 also enjoy San Francisco's best street entertainers who perform daily, the double-deck Breyers Venetian Carousel, bumper cars, a Turbo Ride, and an earth-shaking multi-media introduction to the City's history called the San Francisco Experience. The Pier is the departure point for the Blue and Gold Fleet Bay Cruise, a 1 1/4 hour narrated scenic cruise of San Francisco Bay, and a one-hour Cable Car Company city tour operated by Greyline on motorized replicas of the real thing.

Pier 39

continued

A 707,000 gallon Underwater World at Pier 39 is scheduled to open in the spring of 1995, featuring a 400-foot underwater acrylic tunnel.

Pier 39's shops are open from 10:30 am to 8:30 pm with extended summer hours. We recommend that you pick up Pier 39's brochure at a kiosk on the right side lower level as you enter. You'll have a complete listing of all the stores, restaurants and amusements on the pier. Our partial listing here favors the specialty shops, many of which you may find no where else. Although we love them, we're leaving out the eateries. To find exact locations of the stores and restaurants, refer to a Pier 39 brochure.

Pier 39

LOWER LEVEL

VICTORIAN SHOPPE
Victorian home prints and gifts.

THE DISNEY STORE
This is the only Disney outlet in San Francisco.

PUPPETS ON THE PIER
Hand puppets and marionettes.

WOUND ABOUT
An entire shop of movable toys.

ALCATRAZ BAR & GRILL
You can see Alcatraz while you dine, or buy gifts, books, souvenirs and shirts, all featuring our famous rock.

THE CABLE CAR STORE
Cable car collectibles.

LI'L READER
Personalized books and learning toys for kids.

Pier 39

Lower Level, continued

HOLLYWOOD USA
Home of the stars, a wonderful assortment of movie memorabilia.

KITTY CITY
Gifts for cat lovers.

LEFT HAND WORLD
A variety of items for south paws.

MAGNET P.I.
Decorative magnets of all kinds.

MUSIC TRACKS
Record your own hit song and, if you're like Linda, laugh your fool head off.

POSTER SOURCE
Poster art in two locations, one upper level, one lower.

SAN FRANCISCO MUSIC BOX
Exquisite selection of music boxes.

THE SAN FRANCISCO SOCK MARKET
Socks, socks, and more socks.

Pier 39

Lower Level, continued

SHELL CELLAR
Imported sea shells and shell jewelry.

STAMP•A•TERIA
Rubber stamps and accessories.

SHOWTIME PHOTOS
Fantasy photos of you in costume or featured on the front of your favorite magazine.

CHOCOLATE HEAVEN
Enormous variety of chocolates from around the world.

ONE HOUR PHOTO
Looking for instant gratification? See what develops while you shop.

UPPER LEVEL

DESIGNS IN MOTION
Mobiles and wire sculptures.

PACIFIC WEST GALLERY
Paintings of the American Early West.

Pier 39

Upper Level, continued

PICTURE SAN FRANCISCO
Prints of the City, posters and more.

SCRIMSHAW GALLERY
American folk art.

WHITTLER'S MOTHER
Carousel horses and wood artistry.

KITE FLITE
Colorful kites of all shapes, sizes and prices.

ALAMO FLAGS
Flags from all over and merchandise with flag designs, including patriotic boxer shorts.

THE BEAT GOES ON
Rock and roll heaven - posters, t-shirts, gifts. Way cool.

BEHIND THE WHEEL
Gifts for auto buffs.

EUROPEAN HERITAGE
Chart your family tree. Family crests and background printed and framed on the spot in minutes.

Pier 39

Upper Level, continued

FUN STITCH
Needle craft, collectible thimbles.

JUGGLING CAPITOL
San Francisco's only juggling paraphernalia store.

THE MARINE MAMMAL STORE
Marine gifts, books and jewelry.

THE NATIONAL PARK STORE
National park merchandise and information. The only such store not located in a national park.

SWING SONG
Great hammocks, bells and chimes.

TRADEMARKS
Label and logo merchandise. Cola-Cola collectibles of every kind.

HARRY MASON DESIGN STUDIO
Unique hand-crafted jewelry and accessories. Impossible to enter without buying. Credit their wonderful designs and able sales staff.

Along the Wharf

BEACH STREET

BUENA VISTA CAFE
2765 Hyde at Beach
One of San Francisco's most popular spots is our version of a pub, where the first Irish Coffee was served in 1952. Although some enjoy their offerings of seafood and hamburgers, many just stop for an Irish Coffee, the ambiance and the view of the cable car turnaround across the street. An international meeting place to share a table with people from around the world.

BEACH BONSAI
500 Beach
A small shop that sells beautiful live bonsai trees, and they ship worldwide.

TAYLOR STREET

COST PLUS
2552 Taylor between Bay and North Point
The largest importer of everything from furniture to foods to home decor. An international bazaar.

Along the Wharf

continued

JEFFERSON STREET

BURLWOOD GALLERY
333 Jefferson
The only authorized Lladro (Spanish procelain figurines) dealer on the Wharf. Often they have a 20% off the catalog price. Also, the exclusive dealer of a variety of fine glassware.

THE BAY COMPANY
211 Jefferson
If you're going to buy a San Francisco trinket or treasure, this is the place to look. Large selection of souvenirs. The Wharf is famous for its souvenir shops. This is our favorite, the largest with the greatest selection.

BOUDIN BAKERY
Jefferson between Taylor and Mason
For your fresh sourdough bread. It's worth a visit for the smell alone. Even President Clinton stopped by recently after his morning jog for coffee and a treat.

The Cannery

The Cannery, built in 1906 by the California Fruit Canners Association, was the largest peach cannery in the world. Slated for demolition in the early '60s, the historic buildings were renovated with three levels of walkways, balconies and bridges, all wrapped around a courtyard. It opened to the public in 1967. We've listed just a few of our finds:

STREET LEVEL

THE MAGIC PLANTER
The most comprehensive collection of terra cotta garden art and ornaments. FYI, San Francisco has the finest collection of garden art outside of Europe. Upstairs on the third floor, a second Magic Planter store specializes in fine art sculpture. They ship nationwide.

AMERICAN TRADITIONS
Vintage baseball caps, jackets and jerseys of the teams of yesteryear, as well as other Americana memorabilia.

BEST COMICS AND ROCK ART GALLERY
Original rock and roll art, including original psychedelic concert handbills from the '60s. Posters and collectible comic books.

The Cannery

continued

SECOND LEVEL

LIGHT WAVE HOLOGRAPHY GALLERY
Holographic Star Trek stickers to full-size holographic art renderings.

THIRD LEVEL

MUSEUM OF THE CITY OF SAN FRANCISCO
The best collection of San Francisco historical memorabilia in one place. The museum is open to the public free of charge but gratefully accepts donations to further their educational purposes.

THE POLICE MUSEUM
Across from the Museum of the City of San Francisco, check out the S.F.P.D.'s own Police Museum.

The Anchorage

Across the street from the Cannery is the Anchorage at 2800 Leavenworth (between Beach and Jefferson). It houses another 45 stores and restaurants catering largely to the tourist trade. Here are two of our favorites.

THE SILK HOUSE
Suite 43, on the first level, is one the largest Asian clothing stores in San Francisco. Wonderful silk Happi Coats, Kimonos, silk scarfs, ties, shirts, jackets and a variety of Asian gifts...at good prices.

THE INCREDIBLE CHRISTMAS STORE
A huge selection of Christmas decorations, including theme decorations for golfers, tennis buffs, animal lovers, etc.

Ghirardelli Square

In 1895, Domingo Ghirardelli established the Ghirardelli Chocolate Company at the site of the Pioneer Woolen Mills on North Point Street. In 1960, Ghirardelli Square was created in the European tradition of shops and eateries, with the Ghirardelli Chocolate Manufactory and Soda Fountain still in its century old site. Pick up the brochure.

GHIRARDELLI CHOCOLATE MANUFACTORY
Plaza Level, Clock Tower Building
The ultimate San Francisco soda fountain and candy store.

PEARL OF THE ORIENT
Plaza Level - Cocoa Building
Specialists in pearls of all kinds.

GREENPEACE STORE
First Floor - Cocoa Building
Owned by the non-profit activist organization, wonderful nature-oriented gifts with proceeds supporting their environmental agenda.

Ghirardelli Square

continued

McCORMICK & KULETO'S SEAFOOD RESTAURANT
Plaza Level, Wurster Building
Fresh catch of the day with a view of the Bay. Both excellent.

something/ANYTHING
West Plaza
Contemporary jewelry and gifts. Selection of treasures from local artists.

GOOSEBUMPS
First Floor - Mustard Building
Fun stuff! Jokes, gags, cards, whimsical San Francisco souvenirs.

SPORTS LEGENDS & HISTORY
First Floor - Woolen Mill Building
Restored vintage photographs. More than 1,000 images from which to choose.

CHINA JADE & ART CENTER
3rd floor - Woolen Mill Building
Wide variety of Asian trinkets at good prices.

UNION STREET

Natives call this area Cow Hollow because the primary residents used to be more bovine than buppie (the new word for baby boomers). Cow Hollow once was a green valley that housed the cows that supplied milk to the city, and washer women washed the city's laundry in the long gone lagoon. Victorian buildings soon took over and you can see them now housing the current shops and cafes. If you want to wander through antique shops and small boutiques and sip something refreshing in a small cafe, this is the place.

In the '70s, Union Street was famous for its singles bars and nightlight. In fact, Linda picked up her first husband in 1972 at one of the bars.

Nosh your way down Union Street. All six blocks contain at least four eateries or drinkeries per block. You'll need to take a cab from Union Square (one-way fare is $7) and save your energy for exploring this charming part of town.

Union Street

The 1700 Block

```
                Octavia
    Enchanted Crystal   Momen Futon
         Donato Rollo
         Zuni Pueblo    Kinder Toys
            Georgiou    Forget Me Knots
                 Gough
```

1725 *GEORGIOU* Lightweight summer clothing all year. Raw silk and cotton classic sportswear. Ideal for hot weather packing. Linda bought her third wedding dress here.

1738 *FORGET ME KNOTS* Wedding favors and supplies. Can customize mint chocolate coins with your logo or message.

1749 *ZUNI PUEBLO* High quality handcraft wares. Indian jewelry with an emphasis on turquoise. Rings, earrings and bracelets.

Union Street

The 1700 Block, continued

1750 **KINDER TOYS**
A small wonderland of amusements for tots and adults. Puppets, wooden toys, and an invitation in the window to come in and play.

1763 **DONATO ROLLO**
Avant-guard men's wear.

1771 **ENCHANTED CRYSTAL**
Natural quartz and crystal. Home accessories, jewelry, and fantasy bridal creations. Nice place for unusual gifts.

1772 **MOMEN FUTON**
Custom made futons, (foldable furniture), any size, shape and texture. Wide assortment of fabrics.

Union Street

The 1800 Block

Laguna

Starbucks Coffee Company	Sy Aal
The Mole Hole	Oggetti
David Clay Jewelers	*Anti-Pasto Restaurant*
	Bay Moon
	What's Cooking?
	Peter Rabbit's House
	The Cottage Shoppe

Octavia

1814 *THE COTTAGE SHOPPE*
Country housewares with an English twist. Porcelain pots, table linens, to name but a few of the cottage household items sold here.

1828 *PETER RABBIT'S HOUSE*
It started with the Tale of Peter Rabbit, and now you can collect Beatrix Potter ceramics, darling books, stuffed animals and children's clothing.

1830 *WHAT'S COOKING?* ☕
Looking for delicious homecooked breakfast and lunch? Great hash browns and tasty pies.

1832 *BAY MOON*
Hand-crafted California designer jewelry.

1836 *ANTI-PASTO RESTAURANT* ☕
Tasty Italian pizza and sandwiches.

Union Street

The 1800 Block, continued

1846 *OGGETTI*
Italian stationary boutique. Fine Florentine paper, marbleized boxes and wrapping paper. Gifts, notebooks, bookmarks and pencils.

1864 *SY AAL*
Men's fashion with a woman's point of view. For men who appreciate color and patterns.

1875 *DAVID CLAY JEWELERS*
The most dramatic modern designs.

1895 *THE MOLE HOLE*
Pick up your own Nutcracker soldier and Christmas ornaments in this "every day is Christmas" store.

1899 *STARBUCKS COFFEE COMPANY*
Chic and sleek coffeehouse, originated in Seattle. Muffins, sandwiches in a high tech environment.

Union Street

The 1900 Block

	Buchanan
	Bath Sense
	Coffee Cantata
	Thursday's Child
Culot	Yankee Doodle Dandy
Condomania	Artisans of San Francisco
The Dolls and Bears	Paris 1925
	Perry's
Glamour Jewelry	*Bepple's*
Laguna	

1931 GLAMOUR JEWELRY Specializing in fine jewelry and an enormous selection of amber necklaces, bracelets and earrings. Amber's a great color for redheads.

1934 BEPPLE'S PIE SHOP ☕ Signature pies. Fruit and meat. Breakfast, pastries and coffee drinks. Pick up a meat pie for dinner. Eat there or take out.

1944 PERRY'S ☕ San Francisco's prime Yuppie encounter bar of yesteryear, still famous for great burgers and fries.

1954 PARIS 1925 Art Deco estate jewelry, vintage watches and rings. A great place to get an old fashioned wedding ring.

Union Street

The 1900 Block, continued

1957 **THE DOLLS AND BEARS**
Entrance in Charlton Court - an alley off Union. Collectors' toys, not a toy store. Turn of the century antique dolls and bears. Collectible dolls, such as Shirley Temple, or new collectibles. Museum quality. No touching, but great browsing if you're into dolls or bears. Looks like grandma's attic.

1964 **ARTISANS OF SAN FRANCISCO**
Poster art, specializing in old San Francisco photos.

1969 **CONDOMANIA**
1969A - Novelty shop with safe sex paraphernalia, t-shirts, sex jokes, gag gifts as well as enormous collection of chic condoms. Why not match your condoms to your wardrobe? A tiny store. Lighthearted, not sleazy.

1969 **CULOT**
1969B - Funny men's underwear and accessories. Ever seen a pair of boxers with ants all over them?

Union Street

The 1900 Block, continued

1974 *YANKEE DOODLE DANDY* Folk art gallery featuring one of the largest collections of pre-1935 quilts in the country. Their crafts will make you proud to be an American. Wacky stuffed animals and wood toys.

1980 *THURSDAY'S CHILD* Fun, humorous clothing for children, handmade by local San Francisco talent.

1980 *COFFEE CANTATA* In the same Victorian building is this reincarnation of one of San Francisco's '60s style coffeehouses.

1980 *BATH SENSE* Upstairs - a shop filled with Victorian-era bath pleasures, including a complete set of aromatherapy essential oils and beautifully packaged handmade soaps.

Union Street

The 2000 Block

	Webster
Z Gallery	Kenneth Cole
Fumiki	Body Time
Farnoosh	Uko
Shaw Shoes	Solar Light Books
	L'Entrecote
	Buchanan

2001 ***SHAW SHOES***
Fashion forward shoes for women.

2001 ***FARNOOSH***
European and American women's fashions. Flashy day and evening clothes.

2001 ***FUMIKI***
Fine Asian arts, from large Tansu chests to small antique Imari bowls.

2040 ***L'ENTRECOTE*** ☕
Indoor and patio dining in a French cafe atmosphere. Wonderful fries. Ted Danson and Whoopi Goldberg made tabloid headlines here.

2068 ***SOLAR LIGHT BOOKS***
Metaphysical books and tapes.

Union Street

The 2000 Block, continued

2070 *UKO*
Japanese clothing for men and women. Architectural, angular styles.

2071 *Z GALLERY*
Contemporary furniture, repro prints and frames.

2072 *BODY TIME*
This alternative to mainstream cosmetics offers lotions, soaps, shampoos, perfume oils and colognes without the expensive packaging. The products are biodegradable and recycling is encouraged by discounts on refills. Unscented lotions, soaps and shampoos are also available.

2078 *KENNETH COLE*
Hip shoes for men and women.

Union Street

The 2100 Block

Fillmore

Union Street Coffee Roastery	
Eyes in Disguise	Valentine & Riedinger
Old & New Estates	Union Street Papery
Three Bags Full	La Nouvelle Patisserie
American Girl in Italy	Roamin' Pizza
Tampico	La Cuchina
Maud Frizon	Viv

Webster

2124 *VIV*
Great Nicole Miller ties and scarves. European fashions for women.

2125 *MAUD FRIZON*
Pricey Italian avant-garde footwear.

2136 *LA CUCHINA* ☕
Cute American Cafe serving breakfast and lunch.

2142 *ROAMIN' PIZZA* ☕
Delicious gourmet pizzas - serving 5" rounds with a variety of toppings.

2147 *TAMPICO*
Cases of vintage faux jewelry. Creative cotton knit sportswear (as fine as cashmere) with an easy fit for women.

Union Street

The 2100 Block, continued

2150 *LA NOUVELLE PATISSERIE* ☕
Satisfy your sweet tooth. Also serves salads and quiches if you're interested in health.

2162 *UNION STREET PAPERY*
Fabulous selection of fine paper, greeting cards, customized invitations and special art cards created by local artists.

2163 *AMERICAN GIRL IN ITALY*
This is as close as you get to shopping in Italy and not get pinched by the . . . prices. Suits and dressy separates for the executive business woman or the elegant lunch bunch.

2164 *VALENTINE & RIEDINGER*
Walk down the alley into one of the oldest floral design shops in San Francisco. Housed in one of Cow Hollow's original barns, this urban nursery is an oasis specializing in garden gifts, including hand-crafted California bears chiseled from California redwoods. Where does a bear ship? Anywhere in the world.

Union Street

The 2100 Block, continued

2181 ***THREE BAGS FULL*** Large selection of colorful handknit sweaters for women. Variety of patterns. Like the sweaters granny used to make.

2181 ***OLD & NEW ESTATES*** 2181A - When you walk into this shop, you walk into history. Estate jewelry, vintage watches, art glass and period lamps. The shop is run by Charles and Dianne, not to be confused with Chuck and Di.

2189 ***EYES IN DISGUISE*** Contemporary eyewear.

2191 ***UNION STREET COFFEE ROASTERY*** A tradition of roasting fine coffees for nearly a decade. Buy bags of beans or just a cup.

Union Street

The 2200 Block

```
              Steiner
              Romanticy
              Il Fornaio Bakery
              Pioneer Sports & Collectibles
              Charlotte's Web
              Califia Books
              Coco's Italian Dreams
    Doidge's  The 1887 Dance Shop
 The Music Box  Carnevale
              Fillmore
```

2201 ***THE MUSIC BOX***
Exclusively animated music boxes.

2206 ***CARNEVALE***
Yes, another Italian store. But, they carry women's clothing by local San Francisco designers for the woman who wants to be alluring and have more fun.

2217 ***DOIDGE'S*** ☕
Abundance of homecooked food for breakfast, lunch or dinner in what might remind you of Granny's kitchen. Some say they have the best Eggs Benedict in town. Make reservations on weekends.

2250 ***THE 1887 DANCE SHOP***
Dancewear for children and adults. Grandma alert: Cutest little tutus for your baby ballerinas.

Union Street

The 2200 Block, continued

2254 ***COCO'S ITALIAN DREAMS***
Romantic clothing imported from Italy, including flamboyant outfits to show off your flamenco and lambada. Thriving wedding business, custom hats and veils. In the back, costumes and supplies for bellydancers.

2266 ***CALIFIA BOOKS***
Walk down the alley into a fascinating selection of fine prints and artist's books. They'll even conduct an extensive search for an out-of-print book you cannot live without.

2278 ***CHARLOTTE'S WEB***
Children's bookstore.

2284 ***PIONEER SPORTS & COLLECTIBLES***
2284A - Walk downstairs to find an assortment of sports memorabilia, with a large collection of baseball cards.

2298 ***IL FORNAIO BAKERY***
Italian baked goods for a pick-me-up.

Union Street

The 2200 Block, continued

~ ROMANTICY

(Sidetrip off Union Street for the brave: 199 Moulton St. - Head north on Fillmore two-and-a-half blocks and turn right on Moulton, a small alley between Greenwich and Lombard.) - The store that tells the secret Victoria was trying to keep. This boutique offers the freedom to browse through romance merchandise or view sensual art exhibits in a cozy, private setting. Romanticy's playful alternatives to traditional romantic strategies include silk, lace and leather lingerie for women and men, games, novelty items and a library of books by noted authors on the subjects of love, communication and sexual fulfillment. You can even order a custom-made Victorian style corset. Carol found this store very tasteful, not to mention, fascinating. A real find.

NORTH BEACH

What's north of Chinatown, south of Fisherman's Wharf, and dissected by Columbus Avenue? - North Beach. Also known as Little Italy, North Beach is a sanctuary for free thinkers, artists and poets. This was the birthplace of the "beat generation" and offers a mix of bookshops, coffeehouses, delis, vintage clothing and novelty gifts. North Beach is a $6 one-way cab ride from Union Square, you can take the #30 Stockton bus, or, if you're hearty, take a hike through Chinatown.

Columbus Ave.

The 200 & 300 Blocks

Vallejo
Molinari's Deli
Stinking Rose
Broadway
City Lights Bookstore
Pacific

261 *CITY LIGHTS BOOKSTORE*
Still owned by beat poet laureate Lawrence Ferlinghetti, the San Francisco landmark features an excellent selection of books on social change.

325 *STINKING ROSE*
Named for the revered garlic which is featured prominently in all their dishes. We recommend everyone in your party try the 40-clove garlic chicken sandwich or the party will be over.

373 *MOLINARI'S DELI*
An Italian landmark deli since 1896. Try the king-sized sandwich of proscuitto, provolone and ricotta. Their tiny boxes of almond nougat candy make nice souvenirs for the kids back home.

Columbus Ave.

The 400 Block

```
              Green
        Galletti Bros.
       Caffe Puccini    Cafe Roma
          Postermat     Biordi
              Vallejo
```

401 *POSTERMAT*
This '60s poster gallery is filled with concert posters and assorted psychedelia. More than one million posters for sale!

411 *CAFFE PUCCINI*
Favorite cafe/deli hangout among locals, with operatic decor.

412 *BIORDI*
Like a visit to Florence, a one-of-a-kind store filled with wonderful Italian ceramics (majolica), hand-painted dinnerware, vases, platters and objets d'art for your table, kitchen or garden.

414 *CAFE ROMA*
Excellent Italian coffees, according to the Italians in the neighborhood. Tasty pizza, too.

427 *GALLETTI BROS.*
Shoe repair. They will even cover shoes with fabric to match a dress or handbag.

Columbus Ave.
The 500 Block

Union
Washington Square Bar & Grill | Liquria Bakery
Moose's
Mario's Bohemian Cigar Store
Abitare
Green

522 ABITARE
Contemporary home furnishings and accessories. Chairs, tables and candles. A small store crammed with special items, many from the '20s.

566 MARIO'S BOHEMIAN CIGAR STORE
Actually, this is a cafe and espresso bar serving homemade foccacia sandwiches.

≈ **MOOSE'S**
Take a right at Mario's, then a left to 1652 Stockton. This is the new Italian restaurant in the neighborhood. Fresh pasta and seafood. Tom Brokaw is one of the partners.

≈ **LIQURIA BAKERY**
At 1700 Stockton. Homemade foccacia bread!

≈ **WASHINGTON SQUARE BAR & GRILL**
At 1707 Powell just west of Columbus. Lovingly called the Washbag by the locals. A media hangout.

Columbus Ave.
The 700 & 1200 Blocks

Bay
Tower Records
Francisco

Greenwich
Rosalie's
Filbert

782 ROSALIE'S
Rosalie herself can transform you with her traditional to outrageous wigs. She can also give you a bouffant "do" from the '60s. She provides the spectacular hairpieces for Beach Blanket Babylon, San Francisco's long-running satiric musical revue at Club Fugazi (678 Green Street). The continually updated review is Linda's favorite. She's seen it 14 times.

~ TOWER RECORDS
Just before you get to Fisherman's Wharf, at 2525 Jones & Columbus, you'll find the most current releases of records, tapes and compact discs as well as old singles and classics at this enormous store.

Upper Grant Ave.

⇒|⇐

The shopping continues with far more variety a block east of Columbus. The pace is relaxed and fun with tiny shops. An ideal place for anyone looking for the most unusual or retro gifts or clothing.

⇒|⇐

The 1400 Block

	Union
	Ocean Front Walker
Quantity Postcards	*Cafe Jacqueline*
	Donna
	The Shlock Shop
	Old Vogue
	Green

1412 ***OLD VOGUE***
Popular recycled clothing with an abundance of Hawaiian shirts.

1418 ***THE SHLOCK SHOP***
If you're looking for an aviator hat, helmet, cowboy hat or bowler, this is the hat store for you. It won't be new, but it'll be yours.

1424 ***DONNA***
Contemporary women's attire from Europe.

Upper Grant Ave.

The 1400 Block, continued

1441 ***QUANTITY POSTCARDS***
For the postcard connoisseur, the largest selection available. You will find '50s retro to the standard Golden Gate Bridge. If you've misplaced your sense of humor, you'll find it here.

1454 ***CAFE JACQUELINE***
Delicious soufflés, large enough to share with a friend over a glass of champagne.

1458 ***OCEAN FRONT WALKER***
Great novelty printed t-shirts, boxer shorts, socks with funny sayings.

The 1500 Block

Filbert
Slips
Union

1543 ***SLIPS***
Sami will recover any piece of furniture with attractive slipcovers. Trick yourself into thinking you've bought new furniture.

HAYES VALLEY

Shopping is an adventure in Hayes Valley, now referred to as San Francisco's Soho - an eclectic enclave of stores near San Francisco's Civic Center, home to City Hall, the Opera House, Davies Symphony Hall and the Museum of Modern Art.

Hayes Valley is especially rich in home furnishing resources, featuring new and innovative designs, and is the place to buy the work of up-and-coming artists.

The surrounding environment is not the safest, so we recommend taking a taxi (one-way fare from Union Square is $6), shopping with a friend and not wandering beyond this three block area.

Before we venture down Hayes, you'll find the San Francisco Opera Shop at the corner of Grove and Van Ness, opposite City Hall. It offers a complete selection of gifts for music lovers and all proceeds benefit San Francisco Opera.

Hayes Street

The 300 Block

Gough	
	Ivy's Restaurant
Evelyn's Antiques	F. Dorian, Inc.
EC Studio Store	S.F. Women Artists' Gallery
Coular's	XOXO
Nuts About You	*Hayes Street Grill*
Franklin	

320 **HAYES STREET GRILL** ☕
Excellent grilled California seafood and seasonal salads and the best French fries.

325 **NUTS ABOUT YOU**
Candy and cards, as well as healthy snacks, dried fruits and good coffees.

327 **COULAR'S**
Fun, comfortable clothing and accessories for all ages, including art to wear, handmade shoes and bags.

336 **XOXO**
(pronounced Soho) - A showcase for contemporary Mexican jewelry, decorative arts, and furniture with an urbane, not a folksy look.

Hayes Street

The 300 Block, continued

347 *EC STUDIO STORE*
Stationery and decorative accessories. Husband and wife design team use fabrics in a creative way to create cozy sets, stationery sets, floral pens. Ideal place to select a unique gift.

370 *S.F. WOMEN ARTISTS' GALLERY*
A non-profit membership gallery staffed by volunteers featuring group shows of juried works. Fine arts sales and some gift items.

381 *EVELYN'S ANTIQUES*
Chinese furniture, gallery and warehouse. The largest selection of authentic antique Chinese furniture in the city.

388 *F. DORIAN, INC.*
Handcrafted and handmade items from all over the world. Combine folk art from Asia, Africa and Latin America, with architectural elements and contemporary crafts to create treasures.

398 *IVY'S RESTAURANT*
California cuisine with an emphasis on the freshest ingredients.

Hayes Street

The 400 Block

Octavia
FF&E
Franco Borone
Star Classics
Gough

425 ***STAR CLASSICS***
Classical music, CDs and cassettes.

437 ***FRANCO BORONE***
San Francisco designer specializing in colorful jackets and coats. A design studio atmosphere.

437 ***FF&E***
FF&E stands for furniture, functional and essential. Showroom of quality pieces designed by some of the city's top talent.

Hayes Street

The 500 Block

	Laguna
Mad Magda's	Country Stark Java
Victorian Interiors	Zonal
Laku	Nomads
	Lava 9
	AD/50
	The Magical Trinket
	City Green
	Octavia

500 *CITY GREEN*
A flower shop with something special -- a creative assortment of garden art and gifts.

526 *THE MAGICAL TRINKET*
Beads and trinkets from round the world, African beads, pre-Columbian art and a few local artists who have an international flair.

528 *AD/50*
The organic unity of architectural inspired furniture design of the '50s.

542 *LAVA 9*
Leather jackets and handbags designed right there in the studio. Watch your outfit being made.

556 *NOMADS*
Artsy European clothes for men and women. Unisex look.

Hayes Street

The 500 Block, continued

563 ***LAKU*** Resembles a French department store from the 1800s. A little of everything. A curiosity shop. Local designers offer wire bracelets and necklaces, interior decorating fabrics, clothing for men, women and children, handmade shoes and lingerie and ribbon hats.

568 ***ZONAL*** A gallery store of furniture emphasizing aged patinas. Devotees of fine aged finishes will love Zonal home furnishings. Russell, a former set designer, combines the old and the new, being faithful to his philosophy of reclaiming the past.

572 ***COUNTRY STARK JAVA*** Owner Terry lived in Java, and brought back furnishings and artifacts that are over 80 years old. The store reflects the Java environment and features Gamelan instruments, terra cotta jars, carvings, steel embroidery and heavier furniture including armoires, tables and chairs. One of Diane's best finds.

Hayes Street

The 500 Block, continued

575 **VICTORIAN INTERIORS**
Gary and Larkin specialize in recreating vintage interiors from 1870 to 1920. You can find fabrics, wallpaper, plaster molding and gifts reminiscent of an era gone by.

579 **MAD MAGDA'S**
This Russian tea room and cafe is a neighborhood favorite, but maybe too unusual for your taste. For the brave, an extra $10 buys you a 15-minute tarot, palm or tea leaf reading with your coffee, tea or pastry.

MENTIONS

Our focus up until now has been the primary shopping districts of San Francisco, the areas you'd be most interested in visiting if you had only a couple of days. However, San Francisco is also famous for many other neighborhoods which deserve a mention here. If you have particular interest, or additional time, you might want to make special trips to some of these only-in-San Francisco neighborhoods.

THE CASTRO

The intersection of Castro Street and Market is the hub of "the Castro," a neighborhood a couple of miles west of downtown. The 1880s Victorian storefronts and homes are the businesses and residences of many of San Francisco's gay and lesbian citizens. In addition to the Castro Theater, the city's oldest movie house, you'll find a wide variety of boutiques, eateries, clubs and bookstores. A one-way cab fare from Union Square is approximately $9.

Mentions, continued

EMBARCADERO CENTER

A virtual city within the city, Embarcardero Center transformed eight full blocks of the Barbary Coast into a self-contained business, dining and shopping complex. Bordered by Sacramento, Clay, Battery and Market Streets, the three levels of open air tree-lined plazas, interconnected by pedestrian bridges, house 125 shops, restaurants and services.

Liz Claiborne's first Northern California store has just joined the complex, which also features the Nature Company (a California gift store for nature lovers) and Nine West, one of the best values for fashion shoes.

Located across from the Ferry Building at the end of California and Market Streets, the Hyatt Embarcadero, also part of Embarcadero Center, features a dramatic 17-story atrium lobby.

Easily accessible via the California Cable Car line and BART (our underground railway), this might be a fun stop en route to the ferries bound for Marin County destinations of Sausalito, Tiburon and Larkspur.

Estimated one-way cab fare from Union Square is $5.

Mentions, continued

FILLMORE

A trendy shopping district of restaurants, cafes and boutiques on Fillmore Street has sprouted in the exclusive Pacific Heights residential neighborhood (between Bush Street and Pacific Avenue.) At 1906 is Brian Fedorow, a fashion designer who creates classy separates for women. Also at 1906 is the New York transplant, Coup de Chapeau, who has custom designed no less than six of Diane's hats. Treat yourself to Rory's homemade ice cream at 2015. If you'd prefer lunch, visit Vivande Porta Via at 2125, an authentic Italian restaurant and deli featuring delicious pastas and salads. You'll find hats from baseball caps to fine feathered and velvet at Mrs. Dewson's Hats. Ruth (that's Mrs. Dewson to you) is known as the Mayor of Fillmore Street. At 2185, you'll find a superbly edited selection of contemporary tableware, furniture, linens, vases and candlesticks at Fillamento.

For bargains, you will find resale shops of designer clothing donated to benefit the San Francisco Symphony (Repeat Performance at 2223) and the Junior League (The Next to New Shop at 2226). At the corner of Fillmore, at 2484 Sacramento, is Toujours, featuring exquisite imported lingerie. Estimated one-way cab fare from Union Square is $8.

Mentions, continued

GOLDEN GATE PARK

Okay, so this isn't a shopping area at all. However, you'll find a couple of excellent specialty shops in two of our best museums. Don't miss the Museum Shop at the M.H. deYoung Memorial Museum, where you'll find artsy books, jewelry, stationery, t-shirts and exhibit wares. There are also items of special interest from our Asian Art Museum, next door to the deYoung. Across the concourse, you'll find the California Academy of Sciences, which houses the Steinhart Aquarium, the Morrison Planetarium and the Natural History Museum. Their shop features a wide variety of toys, gifts, books geared towards the natural sciences for kids of all ages. Estimated one-way cab fare from Union Square is $15.

THE HAIGHT

The Haight/Ashbury district, the site of the summer of love, is reminiscent of the flower children of the '60s. Still driven by its youth culture roots, flower power now mixes with bakeries, varied cuisine and outrageous clothing stores. If you've never seen hippies or nose rings, you'll love the Haight. Estimated one-way cab fare from Union Square is $13.

Mentions, continued

JACKSON SQUARE

Bordered by Pacific, Montgomery, Sansome and Gold Streets, this area was designated the City's first historic district. Surviving the San Francisco earthquake and fire of 1906, many buildings date back to the 1850's. The area is known for high quality antiques, interior design studios and trendy restaurants.

At 457 Pacific Street, Limn Gallery offers extremely contemporary furniture for architects, artists and engineers and those with similar tastes. At 804 Montgomery, you'll find an outstanding collection of new and rare architectural books for both the scholar and the layman at William Stout. At 824 Montgomery, Japonesque offers art, crafts and antiques, and, on their second floor, a fine art gallery.

One of San Francisco's trendy restaurants is Bix at 56 Gold, featuring classic American fare. If you have time, enjoy a stroll through this picturesque quarter of San Francisco, famous for its restored brick buildings and gas lamps.

Estimated one-way cab fare from Union Square is $5.

Mentions, continued

JAPANTOWN

At Post and Buchanan, Japan Center is the heart of Japantown. Designed in 1968 as a miniature Ginza, it serves Northern Califonia's more than 12,000 Japanese-American residents.

The Center is made up of three commercial buildings, the Miyako Hotel with traditional Japanese deep baths in most rooms and special Japanese-style accommodations, the Kabuki 8 Theatre and the Webster Street Bridge of Shops. Japanese gardens, shops, restaurants, art galleries and sushi bars are found in this two-level complex.

The Kinokuniya Book Store on the upper level of the West Building has the largest selection of Japanese publications and English-language books about Japan in The City. The Mikado in the Kintetsu Building is known for its kimono accessories, Japanese dolls and toys. Take a look at the antique tansu chests at Asakichi in the Kinokuniya Building.

Estimated one-way cab fare from Union Square is $6.

Mentions, continued

MARINA

This area bordering the Bay on the north end of San Francisco has a Mediterranean flair. It is home to the Palace of Fine Arts, sole remnant of the Panama-Pacific International Exposition of 1915, which now houses a wonderful hands-on science museum called the Exploratorium. Built on landfill, the Marina was the hardest hit area of San Francisco during the Quake of 1989.

The Marina Green, which affords a splendid view of the San Francisco Yacht Club and the Golden Gate Bridge, is a favorite spot of joggers, kite enthusiasts, and on a warm day, sun worshipers.

The southern border of the Marina district is Chestnut Street which abounds with shops, restaurants and services. Chestnut Street is home to O Sole Mio, Carol's favorite pizzaria where for 25 cents, you can still hear Mario Lanzo sing opera from your tabletop jukebox. Just down the block from O Sole Mio is Season's, Diane's favorite party favor store.

Estimated one-way cab fare from Union Square is $10.

Mentions, continued

THE MISSION

Named after the city's oldest building, Mission Dolores, built in 1776, this district is the heart of San Francisco's Chicano-Latino community. The colorful neighborhood features restaurants, taquerias and shops. It's also home to San Francisco's Carnavale and Cinco de Mayo celebrations. The Mission stretches down Mission Street between 15th and Army Streets.

Local artists have enlivened their environment with colorful murals adorning banks, schools, restaurants and community centers. A walking tour including 40 of these murals is offered every Saturday at 1:30 by Precita Eyes Mural Arts Center at 348 Precita Avenue at Folsom Street. Special arrangements can be made for groups for other times.

Estimated one-way cab fare from Union Square is $9.

Mentions, continued

SACRAMENTO STREET

For the discriminating shopper, this seven-block stretch of Sacramento Street (3000 - 3700) in prosperous Presidio Heights is home to a growing number of apparel stores, cafes, antique and gift shops.

Here are some of our favorites:

Sue Fisher King (3067) for accessories for the home. V. Brier (3091) is a gallery store featuring one-of-a-kind multimedia pieces from ceramics and jewelry, to paper shoes, hats and handbags. Try Brava Strada (3247) for Italian leather handbags, art jewelry and beautiful knits by European and local designers. Justine (3263) offers chic French women's fashions not available in most specialty stores.

Fine yarns are for sale at The Knittery (3294). Peluche (3366) offers classic women's sportswear and suitings, and will split the sizes to fit your body. Peluche also carries beautiful handmade sweaters. Dean Hutchinson (3401) offers elegant separates from Canada. The Grocery Store (3615) features young designer apparel for women to wear, even to the grocery store.

Mentions, continued

Finally, dine on the patio or in the Victorian dining room at Tuba Gardens (3634) or go for gourmet Southwestern Mexican food at Tortola (3640). And for the children, Dottie Doolittle Children's Clothing (3680), and her adorable shoes for kids are across the street (3681). Kindersport (3566) carries ski and sport outfits for kids eight years and up.

Parking is difficult, so we recommend taking a bus or a cab from Union Square. The estimated one-way fare is $12.

Mentions, continued

SOMA (South of Market)

South of Market, the industrial area between Market Street and China Basin, is the location of our impressive Moscone Convention Center, as well as manufacturer outlets, discount centers, warehouses, a wholesale flower market and trendy restaurants. The good news is that SOMA is a bargain hunter's paradise. On the other hand, many of the outlets require cash only, offer no exchanges, no parking, communal dressing rooms and are inconveniently located off the beaten track. One-way cab fare from Union Square will run about $5 to the closer-in areas.

These are a few of our recommendations for discount shopping. For more extensive listings, see Sally Socolich's book, "Bargain Hunting in the Bay Area."

In the South Park Area about three blocks south of Moscone Center: Isda & Co. (324 Ritch between Brannan and Townsend) for chic and tailored clothing for women with elegant taste. Jeanne Marc (508 Third St. between Brannan and Townsend) offers fun creative clothes for women - past seasons and overrun 50-70% off retail. KM Wear outlet (625 Second St.) for quality weekend wear for women - 100% cotton knit tunics, leggings and dresses, 50% off retail.

Mentions, continued

New West Design (426 Brannan) offers trendy comfortable sportswear and outerwear for men and women sized 2-12. You'll find leather jackets, glitsy t-shirts, accessories and lots of shoes at the Factory Outlet Center at 660 Third with a variety of stores under one roof. Weekend separates for the junior set are available in some 20 colors, at a discount, at Cut Loose (690 Third). Jessica McClintock's outlet for her feminine lacy fashions is at 35 Stanford at Brannan. A good selection of French and American perfumes, cosmetics and hair care products can be purchased at 10-70% off at New York Cosmetics and Fragrances at two Soma locations - 318 Brannan and 674 8th St.

Just a block west of Moscone Center is one of the largest off-priced department stores in the country - the Burlington Coat Factory (899 Howard) with all kinds of fashions for men, women and children at 20-60% off. At any given time, you'll find 10,000 to 20,000 coats in stock.

A few blocks further west on 9th Street, you'll find City Lights Factory Outlet (333) for innovative workout and body wear as well as terrycloth robes made for resorts and spas. At 434 9th is another cotton activewear outlet, Tight End, and at 430, Christine Foley for handloomed colorful cotton knit sweaters for the entire family. A little further away at 444 DeHaro is the Basic Brown Bear, a teddy bear factory.

Mentions, continued

STONESTOWN GALLERIA

If you're homesick for the mall you left behind, San Francisco's original shopping center is Stonestown Galleria in the southwestern corner of the city, a good $20 one-way cab ride from Union Square.

In addition to Nordstrom and Emporium, you'll discover specialty stores from Williams-Sonoma to Imaginarium, and services such as a post office, salon, and market in a setting of vaulted glass skylights and Italian Renaissance marble.

INDEX

Where it is:	
Union Square Area	pp. 12-79
Fisherman's Wharf	pp. 80-95
Union Street	pp. 96-111
North Beach	pp. 112-118
Hayes Valley	pp. 119-125
Other Areas (Mentions)	pp. 126-138

22 Steps 15
A Pea in a Pod 16
Abitare 115
Academy of Art College
    Gallery 25
Accessories
    Bally 69
    Bottega Veneta 50
    Brava Strada 134
    Coach Leather 32
    Coular's 120
    Culot 102
    Gucci 68
    Hermes 68
    I. Magnin 53
    Joan & David 52
    Laku 124
    Lava 9 123
    Macy's 53
    Mark Cross 31
    Neiman Marcus 52
    Nordstrom 79
    Saks Fifth Avenue 39
    Silk House 93
    V. Brier 134

Accessories, continued
    Viv 106
Activewear
    Bogner 20
    Capezio 30
    City Lights Factory Outlet
        137
    Don Sherwood 63
    North Face 32
    The 1887 Dance Shop 109
    Tight End 137
    Timberland 20
AD/50 123
Adrienne Vittadini 77
Adult Items
    Condomania 102
    Romanticy 111
Alamo Flags 87
Alcatraz Bar & Grill C 84
Alfred Dunhill of London 38
American Express 35
American Girl in Italy 107
American Traditions 91
Anchorage 93
Ann Michaels 55

Index

Where it is:	
Union Square Area	pp. 12-79
Fisherman's Wharf	pp. 80-95
Union Street	pp. 96-111
North Beach	pp. 112-118
Hayes Valley	pp. 119-125
Other Areas (Mentions)	pp. 126-138

Ann Taylor 21, 78
Anti-Pasto Restaurant 99
Antiques
    Ann Michaels 55
    Asakichi 131
    Dolls and Bears 102
    Ed Hardy S.F. Antiques 43
    Evelyn's Antques 121
    G.L. Morris 23
    Jackson Square 130
    Japonesque 130
    Orientations 44
    Peking Arts-Antiques 23
    Sacramento Street Shops 134
    Yankee Doodle Dandy 103
Argonaut Books 26
Aricie Lingerie De Marque 28
Aromatherapy
    Bath Sense 103
Art Supplies
    Michael's Art Supplies 17
Arthur Beren 68
Artisans Of San Francisco 102
As Time Goes By 76
Asakichi 131
Ashling 23

Asian Art Museum 129
Audrey Jones 78
Auto Enthusiasts
    Behind The Wheel 87
B. Dalton Books 13
Bally of Switzerland 69
Banana Republic 62
Bank of America 74
Basic Brown Bear 137
Bath Sense 103
Bay Company 90
Bay Cruises
    Pier 39 82
Bay Moon 99
Bazaar Cada Dia 41
Beach Blanket Babylon
    Rosalie's 116
Beach Bonsai 89
Beads
    Magican Trinket 123
Bebe 77
Behind the Wheel 87
Bellydancer Get-Ups
    Coco's Italian Dreams 110
Bentley's 13
Bepple's Pie Shop 101

Index

Best Comics and Rock Art
    Gallery 91
Betsey Johnson 51
Bix 130
Body Time 105
Bogner 20
Bonsai
    Beach Bonsai 89
Books
    Argonaut Books 26
    B. Dalton Books 13
    Books, Inc. 72
    Califia Books 110
    Charlotte's Web 110
    City Lights Bookstore 113
    Doubleday Bookstore 15
    Hunter's Bargain
        Bookstore 72
    Kinokuniya Book Store
        131
    Li'l Reader 84
    Solar Light Books 104
    The Book Stall 24
    Thomas Goldwasser 30
    Tillman Bookstore 62
    William Stout 130
Books, Inc. 72
Boto USA, Inc. 24
Bottega Veneta 50
Boudin Bakery 90
Brava Strada 134
Brian Fedorow 128
Bridal Supplies & Creations
    Enchanted Crystal 98
    Forget Me Knots 97
    Paris 1925 101

Bridalwear & Accessories
    Coco's Italian Dreams 110
    Escada 37
    I.Magnin 53
    Jacqueline Debray 51
    Jessica Mcclintock 137
Britex Fabrics 51
British Influence
    Bullock & Jones 39
    Burberry's Limited 35
    Cottage Shoppe 99
    Crabtree & Evelyn 27
    Jaeger International 37
    Swaine Adeney 40
Brooks Brothers 33
Bruno Magli 54
Bulgari 70
Bullock & Jones 39
Burberry's Limited 35
Burlington Coat Factory 137
Burlwood Gallery 90
Cable Car Clothiers 15
Cable Car Store 84
Cache 78
Cafe Claude 14
Cafe de la Presse 63
Cafe Jacqueline 118
Cafe Phoscao 13
Cafe Roma 114
Caffe Classico 40
Caffe Kuleto's 73
Caffe Puccini 114
Califia Books 110
California Academy Of
    Sciences 129
California Pizza Kitchen 55

Index

Where it is:

Union Square Area	pp. 12-79
Fisherman's Wharf	pp. 80-95
Union Street	pp. 96-111
North Beach	pp. 112-118
Hayes Valley	pp. 119-125
Other Areas (Mentions)	pp. 126-138

Candles
    Abitare 115
    Candlelier 45
Cannery 91
Capezio 30
Cappuccino
    Café de la Presse 63
Carnevale 109
Carousel Horses
    Whittler's Mother 87
Cartier 35
Casual Attire
    Banana Republic 62
    Betsey Johnson 51
    Coular's 120
    Eddie Bauer 34
    Gap & Gap For Kids 30
    J Crew 78
    Joanie Char 16
    KM Wear 136
    Pier 39 82
Celine 31
Chanel 47
Charlotte's Web 110
Children's Clothing
    Burlington Coat Factory 137

Children's Clothing, con't
    Dottie Doolittle Children's Clothing 135
    Gap & Gap For Kids 30
    Kindersport 135
    Les Enfants 79
    Macy's 53
    Neiman Marcus 52
    Nordstrom 79
    Peter Rabbit's House 99
    Saks Fifth Avenue 39
    The 1887 Dance Shop 109
    Thursday's Child 103
    Ups and Downs 18
Chimes
    Swing Song 88
China
    Chinatown 64
    Crate & Barrel 60
    Gump's 36
    Paul Bauer Inc. 51
    Wedgewood & Waterford 70
    Williams-Sonoma 31, 78, 138
China Jade & Art Center 95
China Moon Cafe 42

Index

Chocolate Heaven 86
Christine Foley 137
Christmas Stores
    Mole Hole 100
    The Incredible Christmas Store 93
Circle Gallery 46
Ciro 34
City Green 123
City Lights Bookstore 113
City Lights Factory Outlet 137
City of Paris 56
City Tours
    Pier 39 82
Cloisonné
    Chinatown 64
Club Fugazi
    Rosalie's 116
Coach Leather 32
Coco's Italian Dreams 110
Coffee
    Bepple's Pie Shop 101
    Cafe Classico 40
    Franciscan Croissant 17
    Mad Magda's 125
    Nuts About You 120
    Union Street Coffee Roastery 108
Coffee Cantata 103
Coffeehouses
    Café De La Presse 63
    Cafe Roma 114
    Caffe Puccini 114
    Coffee Cantata 103
    Mario's Bohemian Cigar Store 115

Coffeehouses, continued
    Starbucks Coffee Company 100
Collectibles
    American Traditions 91
    Best Comics and Rock Art Gallery 91
    Dolls and Bears 102
    La Parisienne 41
    Peter Rabbit's House 99
    Pioneer Sports & Collectibles 110
    Trademarks 88
    Yankee Doodle Dandy 103
Composition Gallery 17
Condomania 102
Cost Plus 89
Cottage Shoppe 99
Coular's 120
Country Stark Java 124
Coup de Chapeau 128
Crabtree & Evelyn 27
Crate & Barrel 60
Creamed Spinach
    Orchard Inn 57
Crocker Galleria 27
Crystal
    Enchanted Crystal 98
    Escada 37
    Gump's 36
    I.Magnin 53
    Macy's 53
    Paul Bauer Inc. 51
    Shreve & Co. 33
    Wedgewood & Waterford 70

Index

Where it is:

Union Square Area	pp. 12-79
Fisherman's Wharf	pp. 80-95
Union Street	pp. 96-111
North Beach	pp. 112-118
Hayes Valley	pp. 119-125
Other Areas (Mentions)	pp. 126-138

Culot 102
Curran Theatre 55
Custom Gift Baskets
    Crabtree & Evelyn 27
Cut Loose 137
Daniels & Wolfson 31
David Clay Jewelers 100
David's 55
Dean Hutchinson 134
Designers, International
    American Girl In Italy 107
    Brava Strada 134
    Chanel 47
    Emporio Armani 59
    Escada 37
    Gianni Versace 28
    Gucci 68
    Hermes 68
    I. Magnin 53
    Jacqueline Debray 51
    Louis Vuitton 35
    Macy's 53
    Max Mara 32
    Metier 44
    Mondi 27
    Neiman Marcus 52
    Nomads 123

Designers, International, continued
    Nordstrom 79
    Saks Fifth Avenue 39
    Wilkes Bashford 19
Designers, Local
    Brava Strada 134
    Brian Fedorow 128
    Carnevale 109
    Diana Slavin 14
    Franco Borone 122
    I. Magnin 53
    Japanese Weekend 22
    Jeanne Marc 15
    Jessica McClintock 18
    Joanie Char 16
    Macy's 53
    McHugh & Co. 44
    Nordstrom 79
    Obiko 26
    Wilkes Bashford 19
Designers, New York
    I. Magnin 53
    Macy's 53
    Neiman Marcus 52
    Saks Fifth Avenue 39
Designs in Motion 86

Index

Diana Slavin 14
diPietro Todd 32
Discount Merchandise
   Basic Brown Bear 137
   Burlington Coat Factory 137
   Christine Foley 137
   City Lights Factory Outlet 137
   Cut Loose 137
   Doubleday Books 15
   Factory Outlet Center 137
   Hunter's Bargain Bookstore 72
   Isda & Co. 136
   Jeanne Marc 136
   Jessica Mcclintock 137
   Joanie Char 16
   KM Wear 136
   Loehmann's 14
   New West Design 137
   New York Cosmetics and Fragrances 137
   SOMA 136
   Tight End 137
   Ups and Downs 18
Disney Store 84
Doidge's 109
Dolls and Bears 102
Don Sherwood 63
Donato Rollo 98
Donna 117
Dottie Doolittle Children's Clothing 135
Double Rainbow 75
Doubleday Bookstore 15
Dreamweaver 47
Drug Stores
   Merrill's Drug Center 19
   Walgreen Drug Store 72
EC Studio Store 121
Ed Hardy San Francisco, Inc. 43
Eddie Bauer 34
El Portal 77
Electronics
   Macy's 53
Ellis O'Farrell Garage 57
Emporium 77. 138
Enchanted Crystal 98
Entertainment
   Curran Theatre 55
   Marines Memorial Theatre 25
   Pier 39 82
   Rosalie's 116
   STBS 69
   Theatre on the Square 41
Episode 31
Equestrian Goods
   Swaine Adeney 40
Escada 37
European Heritage 87
Evelyn's Antiques 121
Evening Gown Rentals
   One Moment in Time 37
Exploratorium 132
Eyes in Disguise 108
Eyewear
   Eyes in Disguise 108
   Rims & Goggles 21
   Spectacles 47

Index

Where it is:

Union Square Area	pp. 12-79
Fisherman's Wharf	pp. 80-95
Union Street	pp. 96-111
North Beach	pp. 112-118
Hayes Valley	pp. 119-125
Other Areas (Mentions)	pp. 126-138

F. Dorian, Inc. 121
Fabric
    Britex Fabrics 51
    Laku 124
    Laura Ashley 36
    Pierre Deux 46
    Victorian Interiors 125
Factory Outlet Center 137
Family Crests
    European Heritage 87
Farnoosh 104
FF&E 122
Fillamento 128
Flags
    Alamo Flags 87
Florsheim Shoes 38
Foreign Exchange 23
Forget Me Knots 97
Forgotten Woman 24
Franciscan Croissant 17
Franco Borone 122
Frank More 60
Full Figure Fashions
    Audrey Jones 78
    Emporium 77, 138
    Forgotten Woman 24
    I.Magnin 53

Full Figure Fashions, con't
    Macy's 53
    Nordstrom 79
Fumiki 104
Fun Stitch 88
Furniture
    Abitare 115
    AD/50 123
    Asakichi 131
    Boto USA, Inc. 24
    Cost Plus 89
    Country Stark Java 124
    Ed Hardy S.F. Antiques 43
    Emporium 77, 138
    Evelyn's Antques 121
    FF&E 122
    Fillamento 128
    Limn Gallery 130
    Momen Futon 98
    XOXO 120
    Z Gallery 105
    Zinc Details 43
    Zonal 124
Futons
    Momen Futon 98
G.L. Morris 23
Galina 74

Index

Galleries
    Academy Of Art College Gallery 25
    Best Comics and Rock Art Gallery 91
    Burlwood Gallery 90
    Circle Gallery 46
    Composition Gallery 17
    Evelyn's Antques 121
    Fraenkel Gallery 49
    Gallery 444 40
    Gallery Paule Anglim 48
    Haines Gallery 49
    Japonesque 130
    John Berggruen Gallery 61
    John Pence Gallery 43
    Kertesz 23
    Light Opera Gallery 60
    Light Wave Holography Gallery 92
    Limn Gallery 130
    Maxwell Galleries 24
    Michael Dunev Gallery 49
    Mosaic Gallery 79
    Moss Gallery 61
    Pacific West Gallery 86
    Rena Branstein Gallery 49
    S.F. Women Artists Gallery 121
    Scrimshaw Gallery 87
    Smile Gallery 22
    Stephen Wirtz Gallery 49
    Yankee Doodle Dandy 103
    Z Gallery 105
    Zantman Art Gallery 46
Gallery 444 40

Galletti Bros. 114
Gap & Gap For Kids 30
Garden
    Biordi 114
    City Green 123
    Magic Planter 91
    Valentine & Riedinger 107
Garlic
    Stinking Rose 113
Geary Theatre 55
Geordy's 62
Georgiou 97
Ghirardelli Chocolate Manufactory 94
Ghirardelli Square 94
Gianni Versace 28
Gifts
    Abitare 115
    Anchorage 93
    Ann Michaels 55
    Ashling 23
    Bath Sense 103
    Bazaar Cada Dia 41
    Brookstone 29
    Candlelier 45
    Cannery 91
    China Jade & Art Center 95
    Chinatown 64
    Composition Gallery 17
    Cottage Shoppe 99
    Crabtree & Evelyn 27
    Crate & Barrel 60
    Crocker Galleria 27
    Culot 102
    EC Studio Store 121

Index

Where it is:	
Union Square Area	pp. 12-79
Fisherman's Wharf	pp. 80-95
Union Street	pp. 96-111
North Beach	pp. 112-118
Hayes Valley	pp. 119-125
Other Areas (Mentions)	pp. 126-138

Gifts, continued
    Enchanted Crystal 98
    Escada 37
    F. Dorian, Inc. 121
    Fumiki 104
    Ghirardelli Square 94
    Greenpeace Store 94
    Gump's 36
    I. Magnin 53
    Jeffrey Davies 25
    Kitty City 85
    La Bouquetiere 24
    Light Opera Gallery 60
    Macy's 53
    Music Box Company 78
    Neiman Marcus 52
    Nicole Miller 28
    Nordstrom 79
    Papermania 29
    Peking Arts-Antiques 23
    Pier 39 82
    Romanticy 111
    San Francisco Music Box 85
    Scotch House 32
    Silk House 93
    Smile Gallery 22

Gifts, continued
    Something/Anything 95
    Valentine & Riedinger 107
    Victorian Shoppe 84
    Warner Bros. 77
    Yankee Doodle Dandy 103
    Zinc Details 43
    Glamour Jewelry 101
    Go Silk 20
    Goosebumps 95
    Greenpeace Store 94
    Grocery Store 134
    Gucci 68
    Gump's 36
Haberdasher
    Sulka 36
    Haines Gallery 49
Hammocks
    Swing Song 88
    Handlery Union Sq. Hotel 58
    Harold's Hometown News 42
    Harry Mason Design Studio 79, 88
    Hastings 30
Hats
    Coup De Chapeau 128
    Hats On Post 34

Index

Hats, continued
    Mrs. Dewson's Hats 128
    Shlock Shop 117
    Hats On Post 34
Hawaiian Shirts
    Old Vogue 117
Hayes Street Grill 120
Health Foods 17
Hermes 68
History Buffs
    American Traditions 91
    Argonaut Books 26
    Bookstall 24
    European Heritage 87
    Museum of the City of San Francisco 92
    Pacific West Gallery 86
    Police Museum 92
    Sports Legends & Hist. 95
    Tillman Bookstore 62
Hollywood USA 85
Holography
    Light Wave Holography Gallery 92
Home Decor
    Abitare 115
    Cost Plus 89
    Country Stark Java 124
    Fillamento 128
    Gump's 36
    Jeanne Marc 15
    Jeffrey Davies 25
    La Bouquetiere 24
    Laura Ashley 36
    Marimekko 29
    My Sister's Garden 40

Home Decor, continued
    Pierre Deux 46
    Polo Store 29
    S.F. Dragonflys & Co. 63
    Slips 118
    Sue Fisher King 134
    Victorian Interiors 125
    Wilkes Bashford 19
    Williams-Sonoma 31, 78, 138
    XOXO 120
    Zinc Details 43
Homemade Focaccia
    Liquria Bakery 115
    Mario's Bohemian Cigar Store 115
Hound 13
Housewares
    Biordi 114
    Cottage Shoppe 99
    Crate & Barrel 60
    Hold Everything 78
    Wallis 26
    Wilkes Bashford 19
    Williams-Sonoma 31, 78, 138
Hunter's Bargain Bookstore 72
I. Magnin 53
I.B. Diffusion 77
Ice Cream
    Cafe Classico 40
    Caffe Kuleto's 73
    Double Rainbow 75
    Ghirardelli Chocolate Manufactory 94
    Macy's Cellar 53

Index

Where it is:

Union Square Area	pp. 12-79
Fisherman's Wharf	pp. 80-95
Union Street	pp. 96-111
North Beach	pp. 112-118
Hayes Valley	pp. 119-125
Other Areas (Mentions)	pp. 126-138

Ice Cream, continued
    Rory's 128
Il Fornaio Bakery 110
Imaginarium 138
Imported Goods
    Bazaar Cada Dia 41
    Biordi 114
    Cost Plus 89
    Country Stark Java 124
    Donna 117
    Dreamweaver 47
    Ed Hardy S.F. Antiques 43
    F. Dorian, Inc. 121
    Fumiki 104
    Gump's 36
    Kertesz 23
    La Bouquetiere 24
    La Parisienne 41
    Light Opera Gallery 60
    Louis Vuitton 35
    Magican Trinket 123
    Marimekko 29
    Oggetti 100
    Paul Bauer Inc. 51
    Peking Arts-Antiques 23
    Pierre Deux 46
    Scheuer Linens 70

Imported Goods, continued
    Scotch House 32
    Wedgewood & Waterford 70
    XOXO 120
Imposters 54
Incredible Christmas Store 93
Irish Coffee
    Buena Vista Cafe 89
Isda & Co. 136
Italian Pottery
    Biordi 114
    My Sister's Garden 40
Ivy's Restaurant 121
J Crew 78
Jacqueline DeBray 51
Jaeger International 37
James Osswald 51
Janot's 70
Japanese Weekend 22
Japonesque 130
Jay Briggs 29
Jazz
    Lascaux 15
Jeanne Marc 15, 136
Jeffrey Davies 25
Jessica McClintock 18, 137

Index

Jewelry
- As Time Goes By 76
- Bay Moon 99
- Bazaar Cada Dia 41
- Bulgari 70
- Cartier 35
- Ciro 34
- Daniels & Wolfson 31
- David Clay Jewelers 100
- Enchanted Crystal 98
- G.L. Morris 23
- Galina 74
- Glamour Jewelry 101
- Gump's 36
- Henry Mason Design Studio 79, 88
- Imposters 54
- Jewelry Stop 76
- La Parisienne 41
- Laku 124
- Magican Trinket 123
- Old & New Estates 108
- Paris 1925 101
- Pearl of the Orient 94
- Shell Cellar 86
- Shreve & Co. 33
- Something/Anything 95
- Tampico 106
- The Shreve Building 33
- Tiffany & Co. 39
- Tom Wing & Sons 61
- V. Brier 134
- Wallis 26
- Zuni Pueblo 97

Jewelry Stop 76
Joan & David 52
Joan Vass 18
Joanie Char 16
John Berggruen Gallery 61
John Pence Gallery 43
Joseph Rudee & Son 41
Juggling Capitol 88
Kenneth Cole 105
Kertesz 23

Kimono Accessories
- Mikado 131

Kinder Toys 98
Kindersport 135
Kinokuniya Book Store 131

Kitchenware
- Crate & Barrel 60
- Hold Everything 78
- Williams-Sonoma 31, 78, 138

Kite Flite 87
Kitty City 85
KM Wear 136
Kuleto's 73
L'Entrecote 104
La Bouquetiere 24
La Cuchina 106
La Nouvelle Patisserie 107
La Parisienne 41
LaBelle 61
Laise Adzer International 18
Laku 124

Lamps
- Old & New Estates 108
- S.F. Dragonflys & Co. 63

Lascaux Bar And Rotisserie 15
Laura Ashley 36
Lava 9 123

Index

Where it is:

Union Square Area	pp. 12-79
Fisherman's Wharf	pp. 80-95
Union Street	pp. 96-111
North Beach	pp. 112-118
Hayes Valley	pp. 119-125
Other Areas (Mentions)	pp. 126-138

Leather
  22 Steps 15
  Bally 69
  Bottega Veneta 50
  Brava Strada 134
  Bruno Magli 54
  Coach Leather 32
  Frank More 60
  Joan & David 52
  Lava 9 123
  Louis Vuitton 35
  Maraolo Shoes 20
  Mark Cross 31
  North Beach Leather 52
  Overland Sheepskin Co. 59
Left Hand World 85
Les Enfants 79
Li'l Reader 84
Light Opera Gallery 60
Light Wave Holography Gallery 92
Limn Gallery 130
Linens
  Chinatown 64
  Emporium 77, 138
  Scheuer Linens 70

Lingerie
  Aricie Lingerie De Marque 28
  Romanticy 111
  Toujours 128
  Victoria's Secret 73, 78
Liquria Bakery 115
Liz Claiborne 127
Lladro
  Burlwood Gallery 90
Loehmann's 14
Lori's Diner and Bakery 22
Louis Vuitton 35
Luggage
  Bottega Veneta 50
  El Portal 77
  Louis Vuitton 35
  Macy's 53
  Malm 61
  Mark Cross 31
Luggage & Handbag Repair
  James Osswald 51
M.H. DeYoung Memorial Museum 129
MAC 43
Macy's 53, 67
Mad Magda's 125

Index

Madrigal 25
Magic Planter 91
Magical Trinket 123
Magnet P.I. 85
Makeup
    diPietro Todd 32
    I.Magnin 53
    LaBelle 61
    Macy's 53
    Neiman Marcus 52
    New York Cosmetics &
        Fragrances 137
    Nordstrom 79
    Saks Fifth Avenue 39
Malm 61
Maraolo Shoes 20
Marimekko 29
Marine Mammal Store 88
Marines Memorial Theatre 25
Mario's Bohemian Cigar Store 115
Mark Cross 31
Maternity
    A Pea in a Pod 16
    Japanese Weekend 22
    Macy's 53
    Mother's Work 50
Maud Frizon 106
Max Mara 32
Maxwell Galleries 24
McCormick & Kuleto's Seafood 95
Men's Apparel
    Alfred Dunhill of London 38
    Banana Republic 62

Men's Apparel, continued
    Brooks Brothers 33
    Bullock & Jones 39
    Burberry's Limited 35
    Burlington Coat Factory 137
    Cable Car Clothiers 15
    Donato Rollo 98
    Emporio Armani 59
    Gianni Versace 28
    Go Silk 20
    Gucci 68
    Hastings 30
    I. Magnin 53
    Jay Briggs 29
    Joseph Rudee & Son 41
    Laku 124
    Macy's 53
    Neiman Marcus 52
    Nicole Miller 28
    Nomads 123
    Nordstrom 79
    North Beach Leather 52
    Overland Sheepskin Co. 59
    Pendleton 21
    Polo Store 29
    Saks Fifth Avenue 39
    Sulka 36
    Sy Aal 100
    The Hound 13
    Uko 105
    Wilkes Bashford 19
Merrill's Drug Center 19
Metaphysics
    Solar Light Books 104

Index

Where it is:

Union Square Area	pp. 12-79
Fisherman's Wharf	pp. 80-95
Union Street	pp. 96-111
North Beach	pp. 112-118
Hayes Valley	pp. 119-125
Other Areas (Mentions)	pp. 126-138

Michael's Art Supplies 17
Mikado 131
Milano's Italian Kitchen 18
Mobiles
    Designs In Motion 86
Mole Hole 100
Molinari's Deli 113
Momen Futon 98
Mondi 27, 77
Moose's 115
Morrison Planetarium 129
Mosaic Gallery 79
Moss Gallery 61
Mother's Work Maternity 50
Mrs. Dewson's Hats 128
Mrs. Field's Cookies 20
Museum of the City of San Francisco 92
Museum Shop 129
Museums
    Asian Art Museum 129
    Dolls and Bears 102
    Exploratorium 132
    M.H. DeYoung Memorial Museum 129
    Museum of the City of San Francisco 92

Museums, continued
    Natural History Museum 129
    Police Museum 92
Music
    Music Box 109
    Music Box Company 78
    Music Tracks 85
    San Francisco Music Box 85
    San Francisco Opera Shop 119
    Star Classics 122
    Tower Records 116
    Wherehouse Records 14
Music Box 109
Music Box Company 78
Music Tracks 85
My Sister's Garden 40
N. Peal Cashmere 50
National Park Store 88
Natural History Museum 129
Naturalizer 52
Nature Company 127
Nature Lovers
    California Academy of Sciences Shop 129

Index

Nature Lovers, continued
    Greenpeace Store 94
    Nature Company 127
Needlecraft
    Fun Stitch 88
Neiman Marcus 52
New West Design 137
New York Cosmetics and
    Fragrances 137
Newstand
    Café de la Presse 63
    Harold's Hometown News 42
Next to New Shop 128
Nicole Miller 28
Nine West 79, 127
Nomads 123
Nordstrom 138
North Beach Leather 52
North Face 32
Notions
    Britex Fabrics 51
Novelty Gifts
    Ocean Front Walker 118
Nuts About You 120
O Sole Mio 132
Obiko 26
Ocean Front Walker 118
Oggetti 100
Old & New Estates 108
Old Vogue 117
One Hour Photo 86
One Moment in Time 37
Orchard Garden Restaurant 24
Orchard Inn 57

Oysters
    Bentley's 13
Pacific West Gallery 86
Papermania 29
Paris 1925 101
Parking
    Ellis O'Farrell Garage 57
    Handlery Union Square Hotel 58
    Sutter-Stockton Garage 71
Party Favors
    Seasons 132
Paul Bauer Inc. 51
Pearl of the Orient 94
Peking Arts - Antiques 23
Peluche 134
Pendleton 21
Pens
    Michael's Art Supplies 17
Perry's 101
Personal Care Products
    Bath Sense 103
    Body Time 105
    New York Cosmetics & Fragrances 137
Pet Attire
    MAC 43
    Robison's Pets 46
Peter Rabbit's House 99
Petite Sophisticate 18
Photos
    One Hour Photo 86
    Showtime Photos 86
    Sports Legends & History 95
Pierre Deux 46

Index

Where it is:	
Union Square Area	pp. 12-79
Fisherman's Wharf	pp. 80-95
Union Street	pp. 96-111
North Beach	pp. 112-118
Hayes Valley	pp. 119-125
Other Areas (Mentions)	pp. 126-138

Pioneer Sports & Collectibles 110
Pizza
   Anti-Pasto Restaurant 99
   Cafe Roma 114
   California Pizza Kitchen 55
   Macy's Cellar 53
   Milano 18
   O Sole Mio 132
   Postrio 42
   Roamin' Pizza 106
Playful Pinnipeds
   Pier 39 82
Police Museum 92
Polo Store 29
Post Office 13, 138
   In Macy's 53
Postcards
   Quantity Postcards 118
Poster Source 85
Postermat 114
Posters
   Artisans of San Francisco 102
   Best Comics and Rock Art Gallery 91

Posters, continued
   La Parisienne 41
   Picture San Francisco 87
   Poster Source 85
   Postermat 114
   The Beat Goes On 87
Postrio 42
Precita Eyes Mural Arts Center 133
President Clinton
   Boudin Bakery 90
Puppets On The Pier 84
Quantity Postcards 118
Quick Bites
   Bepple's Pie Shop 101
   Boudin Bakery 90
   Buena Vista Cafe 89
   Cafe Classico 40
   Café Claude 14
   Café de la Presse 63
   Cafe Phoscao 13
   Cafe Roma 114
   Caffe Kuleto's 73
   Caffe Puccini 114
   California Pizza Kitchen 55
   Coffee Cantata 103

Index

Quick Bites, continued
    David's 55
    Franciscan Croissant 17
    Ghirardelli Chocolate
        Manufactory 94
    Health Food Store 17
    I. Magnin 53
    Il Fornaio Bakery 110
    La Cuchina 106
    La Nouvelle Patisserie 107
    Liquria Bakery 115
    Lori's Diner 22
    Macy's 53
    Mad Magda's 125
    Mario's Bohemian Cigar
        Store 115
    Molinari's Deli 113
    Nosheria 45
    Nuts About You 120
    Ritz Deli 41
    Roamin' Pizza 106
    Saks Fifth Avenue 39
    Sanraku 26
    Sears 74
    Starbucks Coffee
        Company 100
    Tortola 135
    Vivande Porta Via 128
    What's Cooking? 99
Quilts
    Yankee Doodle Dandy 103
Recycled Clothing
    Old Vogue 117
Recycled Hats
    Shlock Shop 117
Repeat Performance 128

Resale Shops
    Next to New Shop 128
    Repeat Performance 128
Restaurants
    Alcatraz Bar & Grill 84
    Anti-Pasto Restaurant 99
    Bix 130
    Cafe Jacqueline 118
    Cafe Phoscao 13
    China Moon Cafe 42
    City Of Paris 56
    Doidge's 109
    Embarcadero Center 127
    Geordy's 62
    Hayes Street Grill 120
    Ivy's 121
    Janot's 70
    Kuleto's 73
    L'Entrecote 104
    Lascaux 15
    McCormick & Kuleto's 95
    Milano 18
    Moose's 115
    Nordstrom 79
    O Sole Mio 132
    Orchard Garden
        Restaurant 24
    Orchard Inn 57
    Perry's 101
    Pier 39 82
    Postrio 42
    Rotunda in Neiman
        Marcus 52
    Sherlock Holmes Museum
        21
    Stinking Rose 113

Index

Where it is:

Union Square Area	pp. 12-79
Fisherman's Wharf	pp. 80-95
Union Street	pp. 96-111
North Beach	pp. 112-118
Hayes Valley	pp. 119-125
Other Areas (Mentions)	pp. 126-138

Restaurants, continued
  Tuba Gardens 135
  Vivande Porta Via 128
  Washington Square Bar & Grill 115
Rims & Goggles 21
Ritz Deli 41
Roamin' Pizza 106
Robison's Pets 46
Rock and Roll Heaven
  The Beat Goes On 87
Romanticy 111
Rory's 128
Rosalie's 116
S.F. Dragonflys & Co. 63
S.F. Women Artists' Gallery 121
Safari Get-Ups
  Banana Republic 62
Saks Fifth Avenue 39
Salons
  diPietro Todd 32
  Escada 37
  I.Magnin 53
  LaBelle 61
  Macy's 53
  Nordstrom 79

Salons, continued
  Rosalie's 116
  Vidal Sassoon Hair Salon 30
San Francisco Music Box 85
San Francisco Sock Market 85
Sanraku 26
Scheuer Linens 70
Scotch House 32
Scrimshaw Gallery 87
Sea Lions
  Pier 39 82
Sears 74
Season's 132
Shaw Shoes 104
Shell Cellar 86
Sherlock Holmes Museum 21
Shirt Makers
  Joseph Rudee & Son 41
Shlock Shop 117
Shoe Repair
  Anthony's Shoe Repair 48
  Galletti Bros. 114
Shoes
  22 Steps 15
  Arthur Beren 68
  Bally 69

158

Index

Shoes, continued
    Bruno Magli 54
    Church's 28
    Florsheim Shoes 38
    Frank More 60
    Joan & David 52
    Kenneth Cole 105
    Maraolo Shoes 20
    Maud Frizon 106
    Naturalizer 52
    Nine West 79, 127
    Shaw Shoes 104
    Timberland 20
Shopping Centers
    Anchorage 93
    Cannery 91
    Crocker Galleria 27
    Embarcadero Center 127
    Ghirardelli Square 94
    San Francisco Centre 76
    Stonestown Galleria 138
Showbiz
    Disney Store 84
    Hollywood USA 85
    Showtime Photos 86
    Warner Bros. 77
Showtime Photos 86
Shreve & Co. 33
Shreve Building 33
Silk
    Britex Fabrics 51
    Chinatown 64
Silk House 93
Slipcovers
    Slips 118
Slips 118

Smile Gallery 22
Socks
    San Francisco Sock Market 85
Solar Light Books 104
something/ANYTHING 95
Sourdough
    Boudin Bakery 90
Souvenirs
    Alcatraz Bar & Grill 84
    Bay Company 90
    Cable Car Store 84
    Goosebumps 95
    Pier 39 82
Spa
    Nordstrom 79
Spectacles 47
Sporting Goods
    Don Sherwood 63
Sports Fans
    American Traditions 91
    Pioneer Sports & Collectibles 110
    Sports Legends & History 95
Sports Legends & History 95
Sportswear
    Episode 31
    Escada 37
    Georgiou 97
    Limited Express 66
    Madrigal 25
    Mondi 27
    New West Design 137
    Peluche 134
    Tampico 106

Index

Where it is:	
Union Square Area	pp. 12-79
Fisherman's Wharf	pp. 80-95
Union Street	pp. 96-111
North Beach	pp. 112-118
Hayes Valley	pp. 119-125
Other Areas (Mentions)	pp. 126-138

St. Croix 60
Stamp•A•Teria 86
Star Classics 122
Starbucks Coffee Company 100
Stationery
   EC Studio Store 121
   Gump's 36
   Oggetti 100
   Papermania 29
   Union Street Papery 107
STBS 69
Steinhart Aquarium 129
Stinking Rose C 113
Sue Fisher King 134
Sulka 36
Sushi
   Japan Center 131
   Sanraku 26
Swaine Adeney 40
Sweaters
   Christine Foley 137
   Dreamweaver 47
   I.B. Diffusion 77
   N. Peal Cashmere 50
   Peluche 134
   St. Croix 60

Sweaters, continued
   Three Bags Full 23, 108
   Uni 74
Sweets
   Bepple's Pie Shop 101
   Cafe Classico 40
   Chocolate Heaven 86
   Double Rainbow 75
   Franciscan Croissant 17
   Ghirardelli Chocolate 66
   Ghirardelli Chocolate Manufactory 94
   Health Food Store 17
   Il Fornaio Bakery 110
   La Nouvelle Patisserie 107
   Liquria Bakery 115
   Mrs. Field's Cookies 20
   Nuts About You 120
Swing Song 88
Sy Aal 100
Talbots 50
Tall Shop 57
Tampico 106
Tarot Readings
   Mad Magda's 125
Ted Danson
   L'Entrecote 104

Index

Teddy Bears
    Basic Brown Bear 137
The 1887 Dance Shop 109
The Beat Goes On 87
The Bookstall 24
Theatre On The Square 41
Theatre Tickets
    Curran Theatre 55
    Marines Memorial Theatre 25
    STBS 69
    Theatre On The Square 41
Thomas Goldwasser 30
Three Bags Full 23, 108
Thursday's Child 103
Tiffany & Co. 39
Tight End 137
Tillman Bookstore 62
Timberland 20
Tobacco
    Alfred Dunhill Of London 38
Tom Brokaw
    Moose's 115
Tom Wing & Sons 61
Tortola 135
Toujours 128
Tower Records 116
Toys
    California Academy Of Sciences Shop 129
    F.A.O. Schwarz 66
    Imaginarium 138
    Kinder Toys 98
    Li'l Reader 84
    Mikado 131

Toys, continued
    Peter Rabbit's House 99
    Puppets on the Pier 84
    Wound About 84
    Yankee Doodle Dandy 103
Trademarks 88
Trendy
    Bebe 77
    Bix 130
    Fillamento 128
    Fillmore Shops 128
    Geordy's 62
    I. Magnin 53
    MAC 43
    Metier 44
Truffles
    Neiman Marcus 52
Tse Cashmere 31
Tuba Gardens 135
Tutus
    The 1887 Dance Shop 109
Uko 105
Uni 74
Union Street Coffee Roastery 108
Union Street Papery 107
Ups and Downs 18
V. Brier 134
Valentine & Riedinger 107
Versateller
    Bank of America 74
Victoria's Secret 73, 78
Victorian Interiors 125
Victorian Shoppe 84
Vidal Sassoon Salon 30

Index

Where it is:	
Union Square Area	pp. 12-79
Fisherman's Wharf	pp. 80-95
Union Street	pp. 96-111
North Beach	pp. 112-118
Hayes Valley	pp. 119-125
Other Areas (Mentions)	pp. 126-138

View
    Alcatraz Bar & Grill 84
    Buena Vista Cafe 89
    McCormick & Kuleto's 95
    Pier 39 82
    Sherlock Holmes Museum 21
Viv 106
Vivande Porta Via 128
Walgreen Drug Store 72
Wallis 26
Warner Bros. 77
Washington Square Bar & Grill 115
Watch Repair
    The Shreve Building 33
Wedgewood & Waterford 70
What's Cooking? 99
Wherehouse Records 14
Whittler's Mother 87
Whoopi Goldberg L'Entrecote 104
Wigs
    Rosalie's 116
Wilkes Bashford 19
William Stout 130
Williams-Sonoma 31, 78, 138

Women's Apparel
    Adrienne Vittadini 77
    American Girl in Italy 107
    Ann Taylor 21, 78
    Banana Republic 62
    Bebe 77
    Brava Strada 134
    Brian Fedorow 128
    Bullock & Jones 39
    Burberry's Limited 35
    Burlington Coat Factory 137
    Caché 78
    Carnevale 109
    Celine 31
    Chanel 47
    Coco's Italian Dreams 110
    Crocker Galleria 27
    Dean Hutchinson 134
    Diana Slavin 14
    Donna 117
    Emporio Armani 59
    Episode 31
    Escada 37
    Farnoosh 104
    Forgotten Woman 24
    Franco Borone 122

Index

Women's Apparel, continued
- Georgiou 97
- Gianni Versace 28
- Go Silk 20
- Grocery Store 134
- Gucci 68
- Hastings 30
- I. Magnin 53
- I.B. Diffusion 77
- Isda & Co. 136
- Jaeger International 37
- Jacqueline DeBray 51
- Jeanne Marc 136
- Jessica McClintock 18, 137
- Joan Vass 18
- Joanie Char 16
- Laise Adzer 18
- Laku 124
- Laura Ashley 36
- Lava 9 123
- Limited Express 66
- Liz Claiborne 127
- Loehmann's 14
- MAC 43
- Macy's 53
- Marimekko 29
- Max Mara 32
- McHugh & Co. 44
- Mondi 77
- Neiman Marcus 52
- Nicole Miller 28
- Nomads 123
- Nordstrom 79
- North Beach Leather 52
- Obiko 26
- Overland Sheepskin 59

Women's Apparel, continued
- Pendelton 21
- Petite Sophisticate 18
- Polo Store 29
- Saks Fifth Avenue 39
- Silk House 93
- Talbots 50
- Tall Shop 57
- Tse Cashmere 31
- Uko 105
- Uni 74
- Viv 106
- Wilkes Bashford 19
- Wound About 84
- XOXO 120
- Yankee Doodle Dandy 103
- Z Gallery 105
- Zantman Art Gallery 46
- Zinc Details 43
- Zonal 124
- Zuni Pueblo 97

ABOUT THE AUTHORS

DIANE PARENTE sets new standards with innovative fashion seminars for conventions, retailers and corporations. Featured in the L.A. Times and WWD, Parente is a Maxi Award finalist honored for her retail seminars and trainings.

Parente is co-author of two books on Universal Style and publishes a national newsletter. The books are considered among the most advanced and comprehensive and are used in more than 20 colleges, including the Parsons School of Design in New York. As a nationally recognized style consultant, she continually advises political candidates, television personalities, professionals, executives, entrepreneurs and homemakers on how to dress for maximum impact.

Parente and Blackman present a variety of entertaining programs: "Shop Til You Drop," "Welcome to San Francisco" and "Looking Like a Million without Spending It."

CAROL BLACKMAN regularly advises thousands of readers about how to live with style. As a columnist and features writer for newspapers and magazines, Blackman covers the social scene, reports on trends to the fashion industry for a national trade publication and writes about celebrities, home decor, entertaining and travel destinations.

Her professional speaking career started when she was a featured performer with the San Francisco Children's Opera Company at the age of 10. Blackman, a native San Franciscan, earned a Bachelor's Degree in communications from San Francisco State University. Her interest in how the human mind learns led her to add a Master's Degree in educational psychology and a California Certification in hypnotherapy.

As a contributor to ABC Television's "Good Morning Bay Area," she presented the latest news about fashion and beauty trends. She continues to speak to convention groups and corporate seminar groups on topics ranging from "How to Create Your Life with Style," to "A Day in the Life of a Reporter - How to Get Your Story Covered," to "Master the Mental Game of Tennis with Hypnosis."

LINDA FARRIS

is a writer and speaker with twenty years experience in television promotion and extensive travels from Siberia and Tibet to Africa and the outback of Australia. Raised on a cattle ranch in Texas and educated in Swiss boarding schools and at Smith College, Farris has made San Francisco and Marin County her home since 1969.

Farris' favorite fun talks zero in on TV tales, relationships and human potential. In "Close Encounters of the Celebrity Kind," she relates her most interesting personal stories of Geraldo, Tom Brokaw, Jay Leno, Regis & Kathie Lee, Richard Chamberlain, Bob Hope and dozens more.

Farris shares her secrets for success gleaned from her search for Mr. Right (and three marriages!) in "Living Happily Ever After, or What Do You Do With Them Once You've Caught Them." Finally, she recounts her adventures in human potential in "I Walked on Hot Coals and Have Blisters to Prove It."

ATTENTION MEETING PLANNERS!
For a good time (and a great program), call (415) 485-5250. We'd be happy to speak to your group.

ORDER FORM

✂

Please send
WAY TO GO! SHOPPING IN SAN FRANCISCO to:

Name _____

Address _____

City _____ State _____ Zip _____

_____ book(s) at $10.95 each .... $ _____

Add 7 1/4% sales tax for books shipped to
Calif. addresses (8 1/2% for S.F. addresses)   _____

First class shipping & handling:
    $3.00 for the first book
    $ .50 for each additional book ....   _____
or
Book rate shipping (allow three weeks):
    $1.50 for the first book
    $ .50 for each additional book ....   _____

        TOTAL ENCLOSED: .... $ _____

Mail your check payable to:

    Buy the Book Enterprises
    P.O. Box 262
    Ross, CA 94957

Call us at (415) 485-5250 to find out about big discounts for quantities of 10 books or more.